Are Pakistan's Women Entrepreneurs Being Served by the Microfinance Sector?

DIRECTIONS IN DEVELOPMENT
Finance

Are Pakistan's Women Entrepreneurs Being Served by the Microfinance Sector?

Mehnaz Safavian and Aban Haq

THE WORLD BANK
Washington, D.C.

Contents

Boxes

Figures

Map

Tables

Acknowledgments

This report was prepared by a World Bank team led by Mehnaz Safavian, under the guidance of Ivan Rossignol, Rachid Benmessaoud, and Sujata Lamda. Principal authors were Mehnaz Safavian and Aban Haq, and the team included Sadaffe Abid, Aimun Ahmed, Syed Mohsin Ahmed, Khadija Ali, Sarah Farooq, Shazreh Hussain, Shehrbano Kazim, Zahra Khalid, Ann Rennie, Jennifer Solotaroff, and Yasuhiko Yuge. Specific chapters benefited from detailed comments from Sarwat Aftab, Imtiaz Alvi, Elena Bardasi, Gregory Chen, Maria Correia, Winston Dawes, Muqqadisa Mehreen, Mario Picon, and Steven Rasmussen. The report benefited from extensive discussion and interactions with, and suggestions and insights from, the State Bank of Pakistan and the Pakistan Poverty Alleviation Fund, as well as various associations and stakeholders active in microfinance and entrepreneurship in Pakistan. A list of persons consulted during the data collection and analysis phases is included in appendix C.

About the Authors

Mehnaz Safavian is a Senior Economist at the World Bank in the Finance and Private Sector Department, South Asia Region. Mehnaz has worked extensively on financial inclusion issues, including micro and small and medium enterprise finance, gender, creditors' rights, informality, and responsible finance. Mehnaz holds a PhD in economics from The Ohio State University and has published extensively in World Bank and scholarly journals. Before joining the World Bank, Mehnaz held positions in the U.S. government, development NGOs, and academia.

Aban Haq is the Chief Operating Officer at the Pakistan Microfinance Network (PMN). Aban has published extensively on the microfinance sector in Pakistan. Prior to her work at the PMN, Aban was at the International Growth Center. She holds an MA from Williams College and an MSc in economics from Qaid-e-Azam University.

Abbreviations

AHAN	Aik Hunar Aik Nagar
AKRSP	Aga Khan Rural Support Programme
ASA	Association for Social Advancement
BDS	business development services
CIDA	Canadian International Development Agency
CIF	Community Investment Fund
CNIC	computerized national identity card
CWCD	Centre for Women Co-operative Development
DFID	Department for International Development-U.K.
DG Khan	Dera Ghazi Khan
ECDI	Entrepreneurship and Community Development Institute
ECI	Empowerment through Creative Integration
FANA	Federal Administered Northern Areas
FMFBL	First MicroFinanceBank Ltd.
G-B	Gilgit-Baltistan
KBL	Khushhali Bank Ltd.
KPK	Khyber-Pakhtunkhwa
MEDA	Mennonite Economic Development Associates
MFB	microfinance bank
MFI	microfinance institution
MFP	microfinance provider
NGO	nongovernmental organization
NRSP	National Rural Support Programme
PMN	Pakistan Microfinance Network
PPAF	Pakistan Poverty Alleviation Fund
PRs	Pakistan rupees
PRSP	Punjab Rural Support Programme
RSP	rural support program
SBP	State Bank of Pakistan
SRSP	Sarhad Rural Support Programme
TEVTA	Technical Education and Vocational Training Authority

Overview

Fostering the entrepreneurship of women is important for Pakistan's economic growth and inclusion agenda, and access to financial services is an important component of starting and growing a business for women entrepreneurs. Most women-owned businesses are small, household-based cottage industries; microfinance products should be a natural source of start-up and working capital finance for this clientele. Microfinance portfolio data suggest that although Pakistan's sector has shown improvement in reaching women, it still lags its regional peers—only 59 percent of microfinance clients are women. The original purpose of this work was to determine whether women entrepreneurs have access to, and are using, microfinance loans as a source of finance for their businesses. However, the findings of the report go beyond the narrow objective of understanding whether microfinance providers (MFPs) are reaching Pakistan's businesswomen. As the research unfolded, the evidence suggested that not only are women entrepreneurs not being served, but also the outreach to women in general is potentially more limited than previously assumed and the issues of consumer protection and responsible lending practices in Pakistan might merit further exploration.

The report raises and addresses two distinct issues. First, some evidence suggests that women are often not the final users of loans, but rather are conduits to male household members. The report documents findings that suggest that the practice of passing on loans to male household members is potentially quite widespread; women may be bearing all the transaction costs and risks of accessing loans, but are not the final beneficiaries. Second, a very low proportion of female microfinance clients are entrepreneurs. The report explores why businesswomen in Pakistan may not be using microfinance products to meet their start-up and working capital requirements, in spite of identifying access to finance as a key constraint to their business operations.

The report focuses on products, services, policies, and other elements of the business model of microfinance in Pakistan that affect both demand for and access to microfinance by women borrowers, some of whom fall into the narrower category of entrepreneurs. The findings of the report are based on

http://dx.doi.org/10.1596/978-0-8213-9833-3

in-depth interviews with head office staff of microfinance institutions (MFIs), as well as focus group discussions with field staff and women entrepreneurs, both clients and nonclients of MFIs. Additionally, the portfolio data of 27 MFIs were analyzed, and a product-mapping exercise was conducted to provide an overview of the range of credit, savings, and insurance products offered to clients. The study is national in scope and covers all provinces of Pakistan.

The report finds that of the 59 percent of women who are counted as microfinance clients, a significant proportion are likely not the final users and beneficiaries of the loan. Estimates vary, but anywhere between 50 and 70 percent of the loans made for women clients may actually be for use by their male relatives. Disaggregated numbers are even more revealing. In urban programs that lend exclusively to women, only 28 percent of the women borrowers, on average, were using the loans themselves. In contrast, in rural areas, where both men and women are active clients, approximately 68 percent of women clients were the final borrowers. In addition, 90 percent of women have to ask for permission from their husbands to obtain a loan, and 60 percent have to "urge" their husbands to repay the loan. Passing on of loans is higher in programs that lend exclusively to women, higher in nongovernmental organizations (NGOs) than in microfinance banks (MFBs), and higher in urban areas than in rural regions.[1] The presence of credit information bureaus can also have unintended consequences: men who have defaulted in the past now use women to access credit.

Against this backdrop, access to finance remains the biggest challenge for a woman who wants to start or grow a business. Women entrepreneurs in Pakistan are engaged mostly in traditional business sectors and still rely largely on informal sources of start-up and working capital, such as own savings, loans from family members, or sale of an asset. Yet less than a quarter of the entrepreneurs identified through business development service providers were currently borrowing from microfinance lenders. Even among those entrepreneurs that borrow, dissatisfaction is high. Why?

Women borrower-entrepreneurs are not able to access individual loan products, but instead are consistently relegated to group lending. But group loans are very costly for a woman who is running a business, and the loans are too small to fulfill working capital needs. Fulfilling documentation requirements, attending group meetings, providing guarantees, travelling, and compulsory savings make these small loans unattractive to women entrepreneurs, and those with businesses to run find meetings burdensome and of little use. The availability of only small loans under group lending causes either delayed investment or multiple borrowings. Even in our sample, which included only women involved in businesses of their own, 19 percent of women admitted to borrowing from more than one MFI to meet their business needs. If a client borrows from more than one source, each additional loan carries its own transaction costs.

Why don't women entrepreneurs use individual loan products, which are more suited to their needs with regard to both loan size and transaction costs? First, businesswomen are rarely given the opportunity to access individual loan products, which are usually offered exclusively to male borrowers, and women are not given opportunities to graduate from group loans to individual loans over time. Unmarried women are considered particularly high-risk borrowers for individual loan products; a future marriage might have implications for the repayment of the loan.

Second, access to individual loans is subject to additional requirements, either of which may be prohibitive for women. Nearly all institutions that do not use the group-lending–group-liability model require clients to provide at least two guarantors. Only men are seen as "valid" guarantors, especially for individual loans, and at least one, if not both, should be unrelated to the borrower. In addition, most MFIs require women to obtain permission and signatures from their husbands to access a loan. Among women borrower-entrepreneurs, 68 percent required permission either from their husband or their family to borrow. Post-dated checks from the guarantor's account or from a male member of the family must be submitted with the loan application.

It is very difficult for businesswomen to find unrelated male guarantors, given their limited mobility and social barriers. Guarantors are often required to accompany the borrower to the MFP, bringing copies of their computerized national identity cards, utility bills, and other documents. In one focus group discussion, several clients cited incidents in which they paid guarantors a sizeable amount of their loan as compensation for helping them.

Do women entrepreneurs have other options available for obtaining individual loans or other products more appropriate for financing micro- or small businesses? Larger loans for women entrepreneurs seem to disappear even at MFBs that have evolved from NGOs and have a long history of working with women borrowers. Bank staff do not see them as a target market, but rather as a market better served by the still-active NGO from which the bank evolved. Women make up only 3 percent of these banks' portfolios, yet across all MFBs, women account for 18 percent of borrowers and 24 percent of total clients.

How does the policy environment affect outreach to women clients or women entrepreneurs? The policy framework in Pakistan is gender neutral, neither limiting nor promoting access to credit or finance for women. The State Bank of Pakistan, a driver of policy on microfinance, encourages market-based mechanisms and focuses on creating an environment that promotes inclusive finance on a sustainable basis. Key strategic frameworks that provide guiding principles on microfinance emphasize provision of appropriate and affordable financial services for all, including women, but do not go beyond data reporting on the numbers of women clients, which are misleading. The *Microfinance Strategy of 2007*, the *Microfinance Institution Ordinance 2001*, and the *Strategic Framework for Sustainable Microfinance in Pakistan* (2011), all of which are designed to provide strategic direction to sector stakeholders, are supportive of women. Indeed, the 2007 strategy facilitated the entry into Pakistan of the Association for Social Advancement and BRAC, NGOs that lend exclusively to women, which resulted in promotion of gender-focused lending activities. However, the push from the policy level has not sufficiently increased the magnitude of outreach to women at the retail level, and women entrepreneurs do not appear to have access to products that foster start-up and growth of their enterprises.

How to address the dual challenges of ensuring that women borrowers are the true beneficiaries of microfinance products and better linking microfinance products to businesswomen in Pakistan? This report is a first step in identifying these dual challenges and in offering explanations and rationales for the emergence of these practices and for missed opportunities. Individual institutions and committed stakeholders should verify these findings, however, to better understand the scope and magnitude of some of the highlighted practices and policies.

Pakistan is one of the most progressive environments for microfinance in the world and is fortunate to have strong institutions in place that can coordinate and push for change. The State Bank of Pakistan has played a leading role in creating an environment in which microfinance can flourish and innovate and can now push the frontier of outreach by setting standards for consumer protection of women borrowers, transparency in gender reporting, and discouraging discriminatory practices and policies. The Pakistan Poverty Alleviation Fund (PPAF) can use its position to reward institutions that demonstrate commitment to serving women and penalize those that engage in discriminatory or deceptive practices. The Pakistan Microfinance Network (PMN) should ensure a sustained focus on women's inclusion in the discussion of microfinance. Through initiatives of the PPAF and PMN, donors can actively support pilot projects that design products for women entrepreneurs and advocate with policy makers for better monitoring and responsible lending practices. An important consideration for stakeholders is the need for caution in creating incentives for increasing access to finance for women, but monitoring and capturing gender outreach only through broad indicators. This approach may be contributing to the passing on of loans from women to other household members, as MFIs struggle to achieve gender targets regardless of whether women are the end beneficiaries.

Although MFIs understand that women's inclusion is integral to the objectives of microfinance, the practice of passing on loans raises serious issues about consumer protection for women clients, and the best and most effective solutions to these challenges could and should come from the sector itself. Designing better products that reach the needs of emerging women entrepreneurs could prove to be good business, achieving double bottom-line objectives. Investing in financial literacy and education of both men and women borrowers can help curb the demand for pass-through loans and help lower risks associated with deceptive practices.

Pakistan's microfinance sector has a strong track record of global leadership in fostering innovations in service delivery, demonstrating resiliency in the face of crises, and developing progressive regulatory and policy standards. The challenges to the sector continue to be daunting—overall outreach to potential clients is less than 56 percent. Addressing the challenges of gender raised by this report will expand financial outreach and demonstrate global policy leadership and the ability to innovate in providing financial services to women. The challenges of consumer protection and effectively reaching women entrepreneurs are likely not limited to Pakistan. By moving aggressively and pragmatically to tackle these issues, Pakistan will once again demonstrate its position as a global leader, pushing outward the frontier of financial outreach to women, and as a model for other countries in the region and around the world.

Note

1. State Bank of Pakistan regulations instruct MFBs to undertake a business and repayment capacity analysis of their borrowers, making it less likely that women can be used as conduits. The operations of MFBs are subject to multiple levels of oversight, making it difficult to engage in indirect lending (loans for the use of other family members).

CHAPTER 1

Introduction

Introduction and Background

Pakistan has one of the most progressive environments for microfinance in the world. Yet, at the same time, outreach to women borrowers and entrepreneurs by microfinance providers (MFPs)[1] is among the lowest globally. Fostering female entrepreneurship is important for Pakistan's economic growth and inclusion agenda, and access to financial services is an important component of starting and growing a business. Most women-owned businesses are small, household-based cottage industries; microfinance products should be a natural source of start-up and working capital finance for this clientele. Microfinance portfolio data suggest that although Pakistan's sector has shown improvements in reaching women, it still lags its regional peers—only 59 percent of microfinance clients are women. The original purpose of this study was to understand whether women entrepreneurs have access to, and are using, microfinance loans as a source of finance for their businesses. However, the findings of the report go beyond the narrow objective of understanding whether MFPs are reaching Pakistan's businesswomen. As the research unfolded, it became evident that not only are women entrepreneurs not being served, but also outreach to women in general is potentially more limited than previously assumed and the issues of consumer protection and responsible lending practices in Pakistan might merit further exploration.

The report focuses on products, services, policies, and other elements of the business model of microfinance in Pakistan that affect both demand for and access to microfinance by women in general and women entrepreneurs in particular. The findings of the report are based on in-depth interviews with head office staff of MFPs, as well as focus group discussions with field staff, active women borrowers, and women entrepreneurs who are not necessarily MFP clients. Additionally, the portfolio data of 27 microfinance institutions (MFIs) were analyzed, and a product-mapping exercise was conducted to provide an overview of the range of credit, savings, and insurance products offered to clients. The study is national in scope and covers all provinces of Pakistan.

This report takes a closer look at two challenges facing the microfinance sector in Pakistan. The first is the potentially widespread practice of women borrowers acting as conduits for loans passed on to other beneficiaries. The second is to understand the obstacles that prevent or hinder women entrepreneurs from accessing start-up and working capital from MFPs. The report provides recommendations for MFPs that will increase access, usage, and transparency for current and potential women clients and entrepreneurs in Pakistan. The ultimate goal is to identify very specific strategies that can be used across the spectrum of financial service providers and to widely disseminate these findings. In the same vein, an exploration of promising business sectors and clusters in which female ownership is high is included in appendix B to help financial service providers more easily identify profitable business opportunities.

Microfinance plays a critical role in the promotion of financial inclusion for the benefit of the poor all over the world. In Pakistan, where financial access is extremely low, microfinance has the potential to increase access to a broad range of financial services. Equally critical to increasing outreach overall is the importance of reaching out to women in general and, particularly, women entrepreneurs. Women's participation in entrepreneurship not only contributes to economic growth but also decreases inequality in society (GPFI and IFC 2011). Bridging the gender gap[2] in entrepreneurship in Pakistan would increase productivity, create jobs, and support economic development, but also increase household investment in education and health, leading to better human capital.

According to Microfinance Information Exchange data collected at the end of 2010, 45 percent of microfinance borrowers in Pakistan were women. This is low compared to other South Asian economies such as Bangladesh and India, where the ratios are 91 and 94 percent, respectively (figure 1.1). Estimates by the Pakistan Microfinance Network (PMN) currently place Pakistan's potential microfinance market at close to 27.5 million clients. PMN data show that, as of December 2011, the share of women borrowers has increased—total active

Figure 1.1 Pakistan's Outreach to Women in Global Perspective, 2010

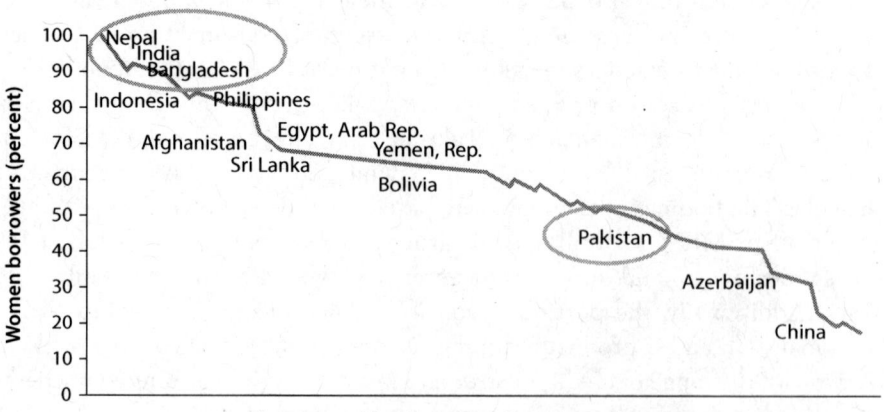

Source: Microfinance Information Exchange, 2010 market data for countries with at least five microfinance institutions reporting. http://www.themix.org.

borrowers stand at 2.1 million of which 1.2 million are women—but this still remains significantly below regional peers (PMN 2011).

Why do MFPs in Pakistan have such low outreach to women? What are the opportunity costs of ignoring this market segment? How can MFPs identify women entrepreneurs and help contribute to the start-up and growth of women-owned businesses? Globally, women tend to lag behind men in access to financial services, although inequalities are more pronounced in low-income countries. Within the microfinance world, however, the picture is usually inverted—female clients significantly outnumber male clients. In fact, microfinance has been synonymous with lending to women; women tend to be better credit risks and create greater social spillovers for each dollar lent to them compared with men. As one would expect, women in Pakistan do remain significantly less likely than men to have access to the financial sector overall,[3] but they also lag behind men when it comes to microfinance. Although in recent years the gender mix in Pakistan has seen an improving trend (from 45 percent women in 2006 to 59 percent women in 2011[4]), it continues to be significantly below global benchmarks, including South Asia and the Middle East.

There could be a number of reasons for this. Some explanations include the religious and cultural differences between Pakistan and other countries. But Bangladesh and the Middle East and North Africa region also comprise large Muslim populations; hence religion and culture do not explain the entire difference. Mobility for women in these countries, however, is much freer than in Pakistan.

Indicators do show that the sector has made some progress in outreach to women. Broadly speaking, women have accounted for half of the sector's total outreach in credit since 2003. Figure 1.2 shows that the increase in women

Figure 1.2 Growth in Microcredit Outreach, 2006–11

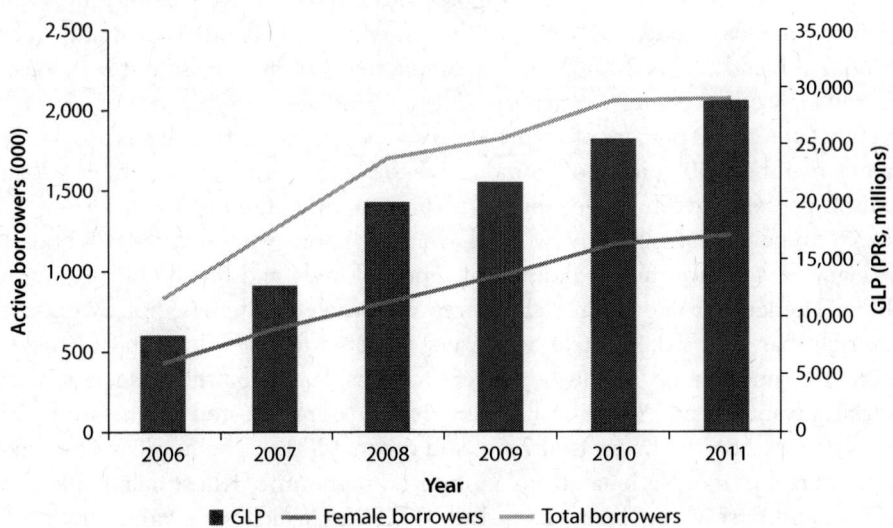

Sources: PMN 2006, 2007, 2008, 2009, 2010, 2011.
Note: GLP = Gross Loan Portfolio; PRs = Pakistan rupees.

Are Pakistan's Women Entrepreneurs Being Served by the Microfinance Sector? ·
http://dx.doi.org/10.1596/978-0-8213-9833-3

Figure 1.3 Breakdown of Borrowers by Gender by the Largest MFPs, 2008 and 2011

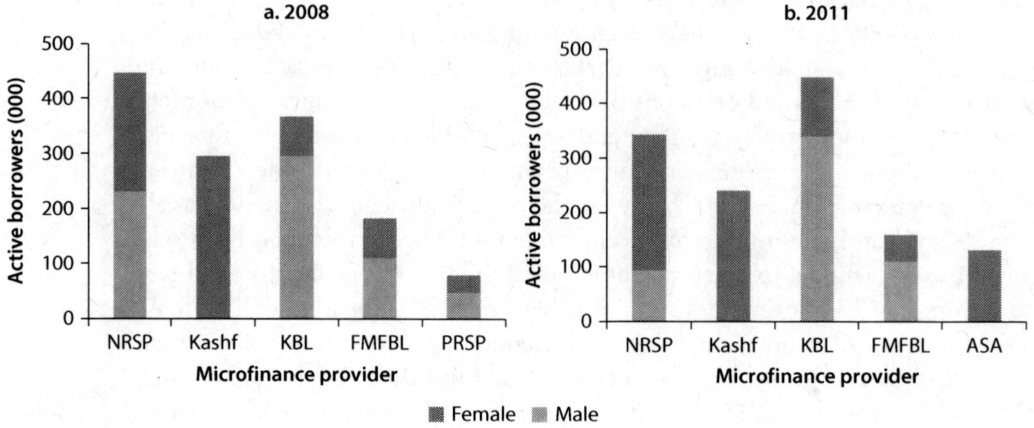

Sources: PMN 2008, 2011.
Note: NRSP = National Rural Support Programme; KBL = Khushhali Bank Ltd.; FMFBL = First MicroFinanceBank Ltd.; PRSP = Punjab Rural Support Programme; ASA = Association for Social Advancement.

borrowers has generally kept pace with overall growth in the sector, and, in fact, more women borrowers have been added compared with men in recent years.

The larger participants in the sector also seem to be focusing on women. Not only has their share of outreach grown, but also two of the five largest MFPs lend only to women, and the proportion of women clients in two of the remaining three increased from 2008 to 2011 (see figure 1.3).

However, these figures may be disguising a startling reality. Earlier research on programs in urban areas that lend only to women showed that only 28 percent of the women borrowers, on average, used the loans themselves (Zaidi and others 2007).[5] A separate study on rural support programs reveals that 42 percent of the women take loans exclusively on behalf of men in their family (Khan and Khan 2008; Zaidi and others 2007). The remaining three-fifths are also not necessarily borrowing exclusively for women's businesses. Findings from this report also suggest that at least 50 percent of women borrowers are passing their loans on to male family members, 90 percent of women have to ask for permission to obtain a loan, and 60 percent have to "urge" their husbands to repay the loan, transferring the stress of repayment back to the woman, who is the borrower on the MFP's books.[6]

Figure 1.4 shows the breakdown of reported male and female borrowers by MFPs. The left bar in each pair shows reported male and female borrowers, and the right bar shows the female borrowers, adjusted for pass-through of loans to men. The number of female borrowers for Kashf and for the Association for Social Advancement (ASA), both urban programs, are adjusted downward by 72 percent based on the findings of Zaidi and others (2007). The number of female borrowers for the National Rural Support Programme, Khushhali Bank Ltd. (KBL), and First MicroFinanceBank Ltd. (FMFBL), which have large rural portfolios, are adjusted downward by 42 percent based on Khan and Khan (2008). Actual outreach to women thus seems much lower than reported data.

Figure 1.4 Outreach to Women Adjusted for Passing On of Loans by MFI as of June 2012

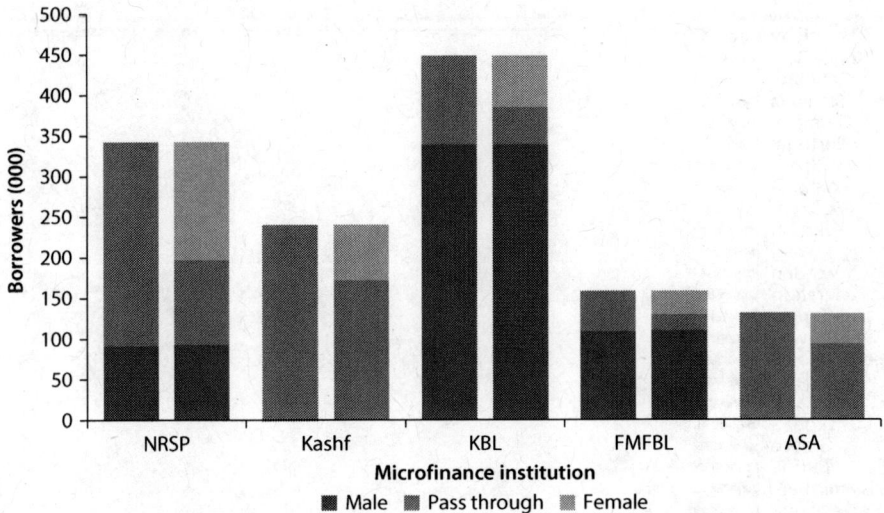

Sources: Based on Zaidi and others (2007) and Khan and Khan (2008).
Notes: The left bar shows reported male and female borrowers, and the right bar shows the female borrowers, adjusted for pass-through of loans to men. NRSP = National Rural Support Programme; KBL = Khushhali Bank Ltd.; FMFBL = First MicroFinanceBank Ltd.; ASA = Association for Social Advancement.

The frequency of pass-through loans is generally well known to staff and management of MFPs.[7] In addition, evidence of multiple borrowing by individual clients, in some cases as many as eight simultaneous loans, suggests that, in more concentrated markets, actual outreach might be 30 percent lower.[8] Thus the actual number of women entrepreneurs is even lower than reflected in the existing data.

Stakeholders rightly point to the fungibility of household resources and livelihoods, activities that make it challenging and counterproductive to try to segregate borrowers and activities within households. This is a valid point, particularly in rural areas, where such activities cannot be practically segmented between men and women or across generations. The practice of passing on loans does not refer to shared borrowing and economic activities that are undertaken by the entire household, rather than by any particular individual. The practice highlighted in this report occurs when one member of the household assumes the risks and transaction costs as a borrower from an MFP, but has no control over the use of the credit and does not contribute to the activity on which the credit is based and from which it will be repaid.

Where Are the Women Entrepreneurs in Pakistan?

We manage to get permission, but it's the money that we don't get.

—Business development service client, Kasur

Pakistan has one of the lowest rates of female entrepreneurship in the world (IFC 2007). Figure 1.5 shows the percentage of female population ages 18–64

Figure 1.5 Women Entrepreneurship Rates across Economies, 2010

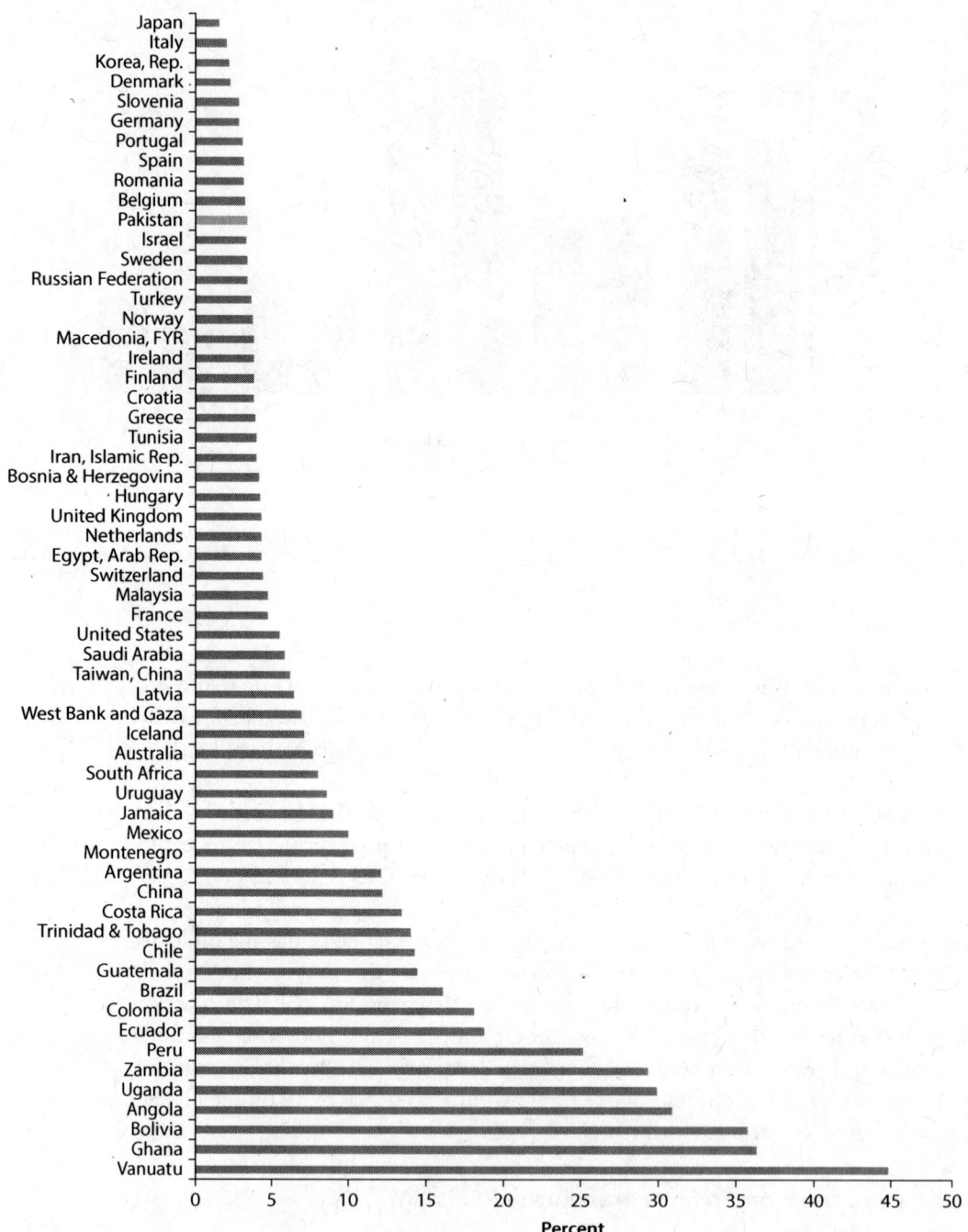

Source: Global Entrepreneurship Monitor, http://www.gemconsortium.org/key-indicators.

Box 1.1 Female Microfinance Market—More than Just Entrepreneurs

According to the *Labor Force Survey 2010/11* (Federal Bureau of Statistics 2011), 13.3 million women are part of Pakistan's labor force. There is a tremendous opportunity for the sector to increase outreach among the economically active female population, the segment that is most likely to be in need of a range of financial services. Analysis of this segment shows that only a small fraction would be outside the ambit of microfinance—nearly 90 percent of women work in the agriculture or elementary occupations and crafts sectors, and 63 percent work as contributing family workers. In addition, 83 percent of them work in rural areas. These women are thus not likely to be the target segment of commercial banks.

---

in various economies who are either nascent entrepreneurs or owner-managers of a new business. The *Labor Force Survey 2010/11* (Federal Bureau of Statistics 2011) placed *female employers and own account workers* at 2.08 million, or 15.6 percent of the total female labor force, but only 0.1 percent of these fall in the "employers" category.

Most women entrepreneurs are engaged in microlevel businesses in traditional sectors such as textiles, food, education and health, and light manufacturing (box 1.1). Although many of these women have bank accounts, they do not differentiate between their personal and business accounts. Over 70 percent of them used their own savings to start the business, and most have never borrowed to expand their businesses. Those surveyed expressed a great demand for business development services and training in areas such as finance and marketing (Goheer 2003).[9]

Businesswomen in Pakistan are the perfect target market for microfinance. Most of these potential clients require small capital to start, prefer service delivery at the doorstep, and are reluctant to approach banks. Women start their businesses on a micro level and usually finance them by using personal savings, selling their jewelry, or taking a loan from family or friends. These businesses commonly remain relatively small. Although a few women cite positive experiences when dealing with commercial banks, most found their experiences with banks discouraging and depressing. Women were put off by documentation requirements, attitude of staff, the need to repeatedly visit the bank branch to complete documentation or follow up on an application, and lags in disbursement. They lack collateral (the assets of well-off women, such as land or property, are often in the names of their husbands), business statements, and records, and find it hard to provide guarantors.[10]

To understand the challenge of tackling the financial exclusion of women entrepreneurs, it is important to have information on the size and features of women's economic activity in Pakistan. The *Labor Force Survey 2010/11* (Federal Bureau of Statistics 2011) shows 2.1 million women are currently either employers or self-employed. This number may be significantly understated, as the survey does not adequately capture the informal economy, in which most women are employed. At present the microfinance sector notionally serves 1.2 million female credit clients and 1.5 million savings clients. These numbers do not, however, reflect multiple borrowing, passing on of loans to male relatives, and overlap between borrowers and savers. Although disaggregated data on women entrepreneurs by size of business were unavailable at the time of this study, it is likely that most of these activities would fall within the definition of a microenterprise. The experiences of institutions that promote the development of entrepreneurship among women corroborate this assumption. For example, the Women Business Incubation Centre was set up by Pakistan's Small and Medium Enterprise Development Authority to promote women-owned small and medium-size enterprises. Managers of the Women Business Incubation Centre had to change their strategy soon after its inception, however, as they realized that most women-run businesses did not qualify as small and medium-size enterprises and were more aptly described as microlevel.

The sample sizes of microbusinesses collected for this study vary considerably. There were businesses that began with an amount as small as PRs 300 (US$3.33) and as large as PRs 300,000 (US$3,333). Among MFP clients, however, it was most common to find businesses that started with an amount between PRs 10,000 (US$111) and PRs 20,000 (US$222), the range of loans offered by most MFPs to new clients. Among clients accessed through business development service (BDS) providers, start-up capital was clustered in different ranges: less than PRs 5,000 (US$55.50), between PRs 10,000 (US$111) and PRs 15,000 (US$167), and between PRs 30,000 (US$333) and PRs 50,000 (US$556).[11]

Most women engage in traditional businesses (see figure 1.6). The most common activity for women is the textile sector, which includes embroidery and embellishment work, boutiques, home textiles such as cushion covers and bedspreads, and knitting. A number of women in our sample began as workers in embroidery or stitching centers where they worked for a wage and developed their skills, later starting their own independent businesses. Other common sectors for women entrepreneurs include tailoring, operating retail shops, and livestock (including dairy). Some women are beginning to diversify into relatively

Figure 1.6 Business Sectors Common among Women Entrepreneurs

Retail shop Lottery packing
Agriculture
Beauty parlor
Factory worker   Tailoring
Vocational center Textile sector
Floral decorations   Education sector
Livestock Crockery and utensils
                                        Food stalls
Shoe making   Jewelry and handicrafts
Photography

Source: Findings from focus group discussions.

Figure 1.7 Key Challenges for Women in Setting Up a Business

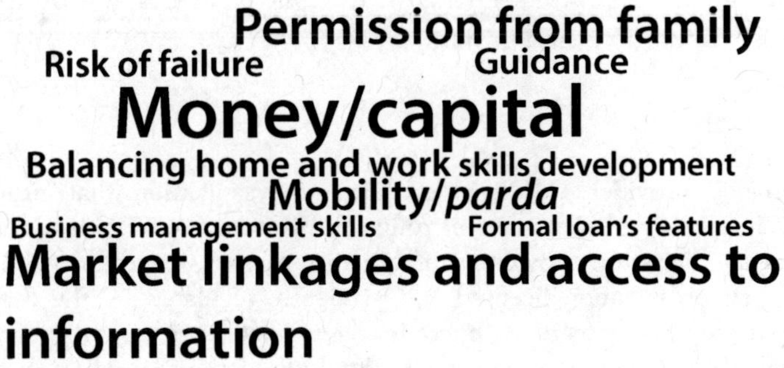

Risk of failure

Permission from family

Guidance

Money/capital

Balancing home and work skills development

Mobility/*parda*

Business management skills   Formal loan's features

Market linkages and access to information

Source: Findings from focus group discussions.

nontraditional sectors such as photography, manufacturing of crockery, and leather goods, but these remain on the margin. Women prefer to engage in activities that require little mobility and minimal interaction with men and allow them to generate income through applying existing skills.[12]

Access to appropriate finance remains the single biggest challenge cited by women in setting up their businesses, followed by the lack of market exposure and access to information, permission from one's family, limited mobility, and risk of failure (see figure 1.7). Most respondents in our sample agreed that the first challenge was getting money to start the business. Once they have access to funds, the lack of exposure to markets, information about latest designs and market demand, and product prices limit their profit margins. A number of women believe that the conservative culture limits their mobility. Even if they get permission from the family (usually head of the household), they carry the burden of the family's "honor" when conducting their business dealings and often have to deal with derogatory comments from other family members and members of their communities. Some women who are starting a business are reluctant to approach MFPs for loans due to the risk of business failure. They fear the consequences of the inability to pay back the loans: "We are afraid that if we don't pay the installment, [MFP staff] will come to our homes," said a BDS client in Gujranwala.

The most common source of start-up capital for women entrepreneurs (whether or not microfinance clients) is generally not a microfinance loan. Only 21 out of 112 clients of entrepreneurs identified through BDS providers (19 percent) had used a loan from an MFP to start her business. Out of these, only 12 relied completely on the MFP's loan; others had combined funds from other sources such as her own savings, sale of an asset, or even another loan from a nongovernmental organization.

A greater proportion of women borrowed for working capital. It is easier to access microcredit for a going concern. Just as for start-up capital, however, women tap into a number of funding sources for running their businesses. It is quite common to use personal savings and business profits. Some women borrowed from MFPs for a large expense, such as the purchase of a machine or a bulk order for inputs, while relying on their own savings and business profits for day-to-day operations and growth.

Notes

1. Microfinance provider (MFP) refers to any organization that provides retail microfinance services in Pakistan; microfinance institution (MFI) refers to an organization that specializes in providing microfinance services; microfinance bank (MFB) refers to an organization licensed and prudently regulated by the State Bank of Pakistan to exclusively serve the microfinance market; rural support programs (RSPs) run microfinance operations as part of a multidimensional rural development program. In addition there are other MFPs that offer microfinance services as part of broader programs.

2. According to Qureshi and Mian (2010), less than 1 percent of women have established businesses compared with 8.4 percent of men, and only 3.4 percent of women own a nascent business compared with 14.4 percent of men.

3. There are fewer women with access to banking services (5.5 vs. 21.1 percent of men), and insurance (0.6 vs. 3.3 percent of men) (World Bank 2009).

4. These data are based on PMN's *MicroWATCH*, which has more institutions reporting than the Microfinance Information Exchange (MIX). Thus the percentage of female borrowers is higher, and different from the MIX.

5. Zaidi and others (2007) use data from seven MFPs, including three MFIs that lend exclusively to women, to assess the social impact of microfinance (the Urban Poverty Alleviation Programme is studied separately from the National Rural Support Programme). Passing on should be lower in programs that lend to both men and women; it is unlikely that a man would borrow and pass the loan on to a woman, but currently there are no data on loan utilization rates in programs that lend to both men and women.

6. Studies from other South Asian countries also confirm the high prevalence of this phenomenon. For example, Hunt and Kasynathan (2002, 20) look at three nongovernmental organizations in Bangladesh and one in India and find that "only a minority of women receiving credit from poverty-oriented microfinance programmes are controlling their loans"; Goetz and Sen Gupta (1996) found that, on average, only 37 percent of loans provided by four different Bangladeshi credit organizations were either fully or significantly controlled by women.

7. For example, Asasah lends exclusively to women. Yet due to the passing on of loans, Asasah requires signatures from both its client and her spouse to ensure that the man understands that he has an obligation to pay back the loan along with his wife and that the burden of repayment is not the woman's alone. The policy might be gender friendly in spirit, but it is paradoxical that an institution that claims to lend only to women, and reports its clients as women, is aware that a significant portion of these loans are actually used by men.

8. Outreach is measured by the number of active borrowers. In practice, however, MFPs use the number of active loans as a proxy for the number of borrowers. Thus if a borrower has loans from multiple MFPs and each MFP reports her as a borrower, the number of individual women being served would be lower than reported due to double (or multiple) counting.

9. This study was based on a sample of 150 women entrepreneurs in three large cities of Pakistan: Islamabad, Rawalpindi, and Lahore. The demand for business support services appears repeatedly in studies on women entrepreneurs. Gine and Mansuri (2013) test whether it is lack of credit or lack of skills that constrains businesses through a randomized controlled trial in Pakistan's Punjab. They find that business training improves the business knowledge of both men and women. The improvement carries through time even after a lapse of one-and-a-half years. Training also has a positive effect on business practices and household outcomes, but most of the benefit went to men and little to women. It also decreases the rate of business failure among men, but not among women. Access to larger loans, however, has little effect on either men or women.

10. These findings are generally corroborated by other studies such as Roomi and Parrott (2008) and Goheer (2003).

11. Data presented here on amount and source of start-up capital, type of economic activity, and challenges for women entrepreneurs were collected from both MFP clients and BDS clients during focus group discussions. For details about methodology, refer to appendix A.

12. Existing business clusters offer a ripe market for microfinance providers. See appendix B for more discussion on this topic and details about two key clusters in which women's participation is high.

References

Federal Bureau of Statistics. 2011. *Labor Force Survey 2010/11*. Government of Pakistan, Statistics Division, Federal Bureau of Statistics, Islamabad, Pakistan.

Gine, Xavier, and Ghazala Mansuri. 2013. *Money or Ideas? A Field Experiment on Constraints to Entrepreneurship in Rural Pakistan*. Mimeo, World Bank.

Goetz, Anne M., and Rina Sen Gupta. 1996. "Who Takes the Credit? Gender, Power, and Control over Loan Use in Rural Credit Programmes in Bangladesh." *World Development* 24 (1): 45–63.

Goheer, Nabeel A. 2003. *Women Entrepreneurs in Pakistan: How to Increase Their Bargaining Power*. Geneva: International Labour Office.

GPFI (Global Partnership for Financial Inclusion) and IFC (International Finance Corp.). 2011. *Strengthening Access to Finance for Women-Owned SMEs in Developing Countries*. Washington, DC: GPFI.

Hunt, Juliet, and Nalini Kasynathan. 2002. "Reflections on Microfinance and Women's Empowerment." *Development Bulletin* 57: 71–5.

IFC (International Finance Corp.). 2007. *Gender Entrepreneurship Markets. Country Brief: Pakistan*. Washington, DC: IFC.

Khan, Shaheen R., and Shahrukh R. Khan. 2008. *Women's Access to and Control over Micro Credit in Rural Support Programme (RSP) Areas*. Islamabad: Rural Support Programmes Network.

PMN (Pakistan Microfinance Network). 2006. *MicroWATCH* 1 (October). http://www.microfinanceconnect.info/user_articles_display.php?sno=41.

———. 2007. *MicroWATCH* 6 (January–December). http://www.microfinanceconnect.info/user_articles_display.php?sno=41.

————. 2008. *MicroWATCH* 10 (October–December). http://www.microfinanceconnect
.info/user_articles_display.php?sno=41.

————. 2009. *MicroWATCH* 14 (January–December). http://www.microfinanceconnect
.info/user_articles_display.php?sno=41.

————. 2010. *MicroWATCH* 18 (January–December). http://www.microfinanceconnect
.info/user_articles_display.php?sno=41.

————. 2011. *MicroWATCH* 22 (October–December). http://www.scribd.com/doc
/86644843/Micro-Watch-Issue-22.

Qureshi, Shahid, and Sarfraz Mian. 2010. *Global Entrepreneurship Monitor—Pakistan.*
Karachi, Pakistan: Institute of Business Administration.

Roomi, Muhammad A., and Guy Parrott. 2008. "Barriers to Development and Progression
of Women Entrepreneurs in Pakistan." *Journal of Entrepreneurship* 17: 59.

World Bank. 2009. *Bringing Finance to Pakistan's Poor: The International Bank for Recon-
struction and Development.* Washington, DC: World Bank.

Zaidi, S. Akbar, Haroon Jamal, Sarah Javeed, and Sarah Zaka. 2007. *Social Impact
Assessment of Microfinance Programmes.* Draft report, European Union-Pakistan
Financial Services Sector Reform Programme, Islamabad.

CHAPTER 2

Findings from Focus Group Discussions

Chapter 1 presented evidence that outreach by microfinance providers (MFPs) to women is extremely limited, more so than the current published data suggest. Furthermore, the number of women entrepreneurs who benefit from MFP loans is even more limited. A series of focus group discussions was conducted in an attempt to understand why. Extensive interviews with MFP clients, loan officers, middle and senior management, and donors show the ways in which products and processes exclude women, encourage women to borrow on behalf of male family members, or create such high transaction costs as to dissuade any successful entrepreneur from borrowing.

Group-lending models impose significant opportunity costs on clients through compulsory meetings and management of the group's credit discipline. Most men are unwilling to tolerate such requirements and use women as a conduit for obtaining loans for their own businesses. For women engaged in businesses of their own, these costs are high compared to the sizes of the loans, which often need to be supplemented with other sources of funds. Larger individual loans require guarantees that are extremely difficult for women borrowers to provide, thus excluding them. Attitudes within MFPs also show that the concept of "entrepreneurship" is automatically associated with men rather than women.[1]

Data Collection and Analysis

In this study, microfinance includes credit, savings, and insurance services. The study focuses exclusively on women entrepreneurs and their access to the range of financial services offered by MFPs. The terms client, borrower, and entrepreneur, which are often used interchangeably in microfinance, are separately defined. A *client* has taken a loan, saved with an MFP, or obtained microinsurance. A *borrower* has obtained a loan from an MFP. Most important is the distinction between a *borrower* and an *entrepreneur*. Both research and practical experience show that not all borrowers are entrepreneurs; this is truer for women than for men. For the purposes of this study, any woman who is self-employed or employs up to 10 people is considered an entrepreneur.[2]

The main tools for the study included in-depth interviews with head office staff of MFPs and focus group discussions with field staff as well as with active female microfinance borrowers and entrepreneurs. In addition, the portfolio data of 27 MFPs were analyzed to obtain information on female borrowers, indicators of portfolio quality across the gender divide, and any other institution-level data that could facilitate analysis and study design. A desk-based product-mapping analysis of 27 MFPs was used to get a bird's-eye view of the credit, savings, and insurance products that were being offered in the market and their main features. A review of policy documents and discussions with key stakeholders and donors were undertaken to complement the findings from the field and understand the policy environment.

The study is national in its scope and covers all provinces of Pakistan. Within a province, selection of districts for analysis was driven by the level of microfinance activity: microfinance penetration is higher in regions with greater economic activity and opportunity, regions in which the presence of women entrepreneurs is more likely. Rural as well as urban locations were chosen.

Thirty-three focus group discussions were conducted with 227 clients. MFPs provided the names of nearly 50 percent of the respondents, and the rest were identified with the assistance of organizations that provide business development services (BDS) or skills training to women microentrepreneurs. Identifying respondents through business development and skills training providers enabled the study to include the perspective of entrepreneurs who may not be users of microcredit services. Fifteen focus group discussions were organized with 82 MFP field staff members. Most of these were loan officers; a few were branch managers (figure 2.1). (For detailed methodology, see appendix A.)

Figure 2.1 Distribution Sample of Women Entrepreneurs and Field Staff by Type of Microfinance Provider

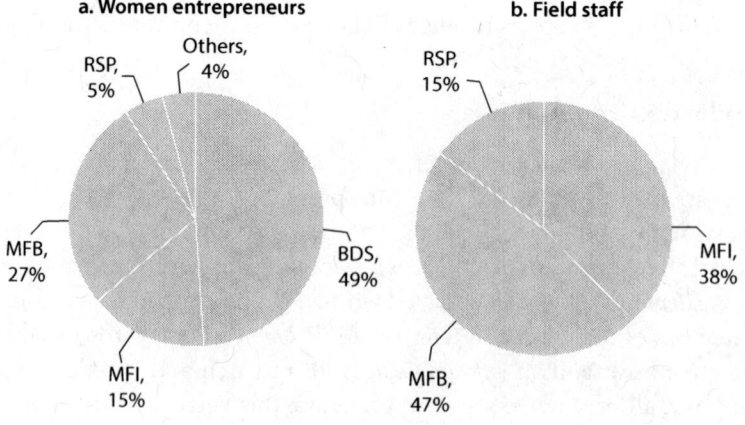

Source: World Bank Data
Note: BDS = business development services; MFB = microfinance bank; MFI = microfinance institution; RSP = rural support program.

Findings from Focus Group Discussions: Pass-Through Lending

Often men borrow from multiple sources and their [credit information bureau report] is negative, so they borrow through females.

—Interview with head office staff of a microfinance bank

Previous studies have shown that a large proportion of women clients are not the final beneficiaries of their loans. No recent data collection effort identifies the exact scope and magnitude of this problem. According to the interviews conducted for this report, however, 46 percent of head office staff and 35 percent of field staff believed that at least 50 percent of loans to women were used by someone other than the nominal borrower. Head office staff are aware that men are the beneficiaries of a large number of loans, but this is seen as a tactic for making a husband jointly responsible for repayment. Detailed surveys on the allocation of resources within households might provide additional insight into this problem.

The passing on of loans seems to be driven by a number of factors. Loans made by institutions that lend only to women are passed on more often than loans made by other MFPs. Men also face constraints in raising capital; women become a source of formal financing when the supply of credit to men is reduced.

Men are unwilling to bear the transaction costs (time spent forming groups and attending group meetings) and the opportunity costs (income lost from time spent away from their businesses) associated with microfinance. But they often need the loan. The woman used as a conduit bears the transaction costs and the risks, but is not using the money herself.

The absence of systems within MFPs to confirm the actual beneficiary of the loan and tolerance of the passing on of loans enable loan officers and field staff to lend without concern for the identity of the loan's ultimate user. Evidence also shows that head office staff are aware that loans are passed on, but seem satisfied if the loan is used within the family. When strong emphasis is laid on the borrower's being the user of the funds, the proportion of female borrowing in the total portfolio tends to be lower, a much more accurate barometer of outreach to women.

The introduction of credit information bureaus and the use of computerized national identity cards as a unique personal identifier appear to show that men who have defaulted on their own loans in the past are using female members of their families to gain access to loans.

Because of social values and prevailing patriarchal roles, the needs of a man's business are placed before those of a woman's business in the household. For example, if a woman's son is unemployed, the loan is more likely to be given to him to finance some economic activity than to the woman to enable her to start her own business. Women's businesses also tend to have lower returns; it can make economic sense to divert the additional resources into a man's business.

A silver lining in this scenario is the finding that women who have taken on three or four loans begin to think of how they can use the money for their own economic activity. The process of obtaining financing, even if initially on behalf of a male relative, creates an awareness of the possibilities that exist for them.

Findings from Focus Group Discussions: Credit for Entrepreneurship

A male member of the family has to be present at the time the loan is handed to a client. Their assurance has to be given to the bank.

—Focus group discussion with clients of a microfinance bank, Hyderabad

They have to beg to get the guarantee.

—Focus group discussion with microfinance institution field staff, Kasur

A significant proportion of women entrepreneurs choose not to borrow from MFPs. Less than a quarter of the entrepreneurs (23 percent) identified through BDS providers were borrowing from MFPs. A small proportion (4 percent) borrow from other formal sources such as commercial banks, and the rest rely for capital on own savings, loans from family members, or profit from their businesses. Many women find the group-lending products available through MFPs unsuitable for their needs. Individual loan products are rarely offered to women; those that are come with onerous guarantor requirements that effectively preclude their use. Some fear the consequences of their inability to repay the loan. Few cited lack of information. Even among those entrepreneurs that do borrow, dissatisfaction is high.

Group lending, the predominant methodology for lending to women (under which the group is responsible for the payment of each individual borrower's loan), generally places a limit on loan size. The average loan is PRs 30,000 (US$333), beyond which groups tend to break down, as clients with smaller loans may be reluctant to take on the risk of guaranteeing the repayment of larger loans. For women with established businesses, this amount is no longer sufficient. The situation is exacerbated by the often-small increment that a client receives from one loan cycle to the next. Business investments must be delayed or money must be borrowed from other sources. Even in this sample, which included only women involved in businesses of their own, 19 percent of women admitted to borrowing from more than one MFP to meet their business needs. Group meetings also impose opportunity costs for women entrepreneurs. Those with businesses to run find meetings burdensome and of little use. For example, a group meeting can be short if all members are present with accurate repayments, but generally lasts for three to four hours, causing a loss of at least half a day of work. Transaction costs for group loans also make them unattractive: fulfilling documentation requirements and maintaining credit discipline in groups do not seem worthwhile to women who have a business to run. If a client has borrowed from more than one source, the transaction costs can be quite significant.

Even among women entrepreneurs who use group-lending products, 68 percent required permission either from their husband or their family to borrow. MFPs, with few exceptions, require women to obtain their husband's consent and signature for processing a loan. Clients and field staff make clear that a woman cannot obtain a loan without her husband's (or male head of the family's) permission. Field staff consider the husband, as opposed to the lending group, to be the real guarantor of the loan.

Group lending is an important part of microfinance lending activity and is an appropriate means of access to credit for certain women, especially in rural areas. Group lending is a model for leveraging small loans within a community and helps build social cohesion. Its use is more limited, however, for borrowers who plan to expand a microenterprise, particularly in urban areas where social cohesion is weaker, making it more difficult to control the group. For example, 80 percent of the women entrepreneurs interviewed through BDS providers believe that group lending is problematic and does not suit their needs. Opportunity and transaction costs of participation are high, and maintaining credit discipline within the group is difficult (figure 2.2). Women entrepreneurs need more options.

Why don't women microentrepreneurs use the individual loan products, whose size and transaction costs are suitable for micro- and small business activities, offered by Pakistan's MFPs? Individual lending offers the greatest range and the most flexibility, but women rarely borrow individually (only 9 percent of women borrow as individuals compared to 17 percent of men). One reason is that guarantor requirements for individual loans may be prohibitive for women. Nearly all institutions that offer individual loans require clients to provide at least two guarantors (see box 2.1). Only men are seen as "valid" guarantors, especially for individual loans, and at least one, if not both, should be unrelated to the borrower. Post-dated checks from the guarantor's account (or from a male member of the family) must be submitted with the loan application. It is very difficult for

Figure 2.2 Issues with Existing Model for Lending to Women Entrepreneurs in Pakistan

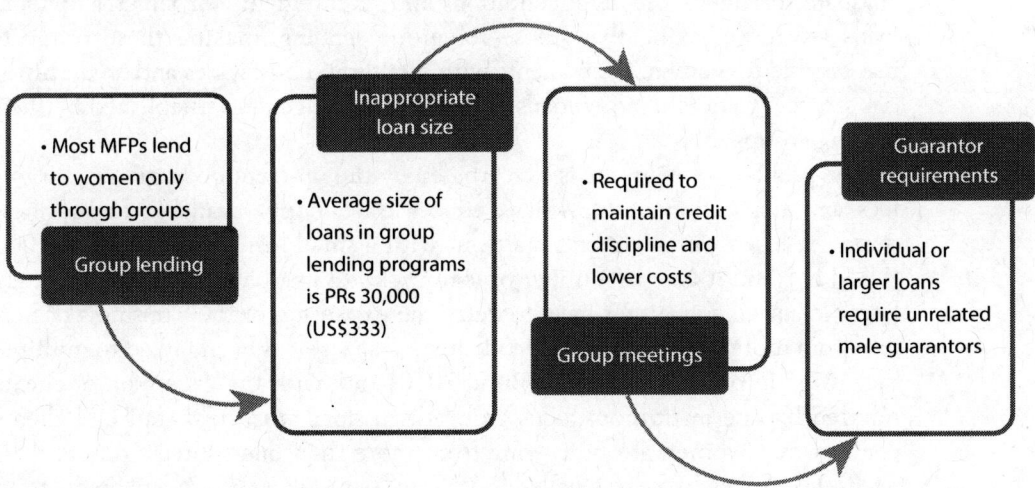

Note: MFP = microfinance provider; PRs = Pakistan rupees.

Box 2.1 Types of Guarantees Required for Individual Loans

- Two male guarantors, only one of whom can be from the borrower's immediate family
- Signature of a male family member
- Personal guarantee from someone who is a public- or private-sector employee with a protected salary, a person with an independent business (such as a doctor or shopkeeper), or a person running a microenterprise with monthly net income (after all household and business expenses are met) at least equal to the total amount of the monthly loan installment of the borrower
- One personal guarantor with positive cash flow plus post-dated checks provided by the borrower
- Two guarantors who are financially independent and permanent residents of the same territory plus post-dated checks and other documentation, such as promissory notes and stamp paper to be submitted by the borrower

women to find male guarantors who are not relatives, given their limited mobility and social barriers. In one focus group discussion, clients cited incidents in which they paid guarantors a sizeable amount of their loan as compensation for helping them. Some institutions have made the guarantor requirement explicit and formal, whereas others do not have a written policy. Irrespective of whether the requirement is formal or informal, the preference for a male guarantor is clearly understood by the field staff as well as by clients.

If women entrepreneurs who initially participate in group lending could graduate to larger loans and individual products over time, the perceived payoffs of those loans and more individualized products would make the costs of participating in group lending less onerous. In general, only male borrowers are able to take advantage of the range of loan sizes on offer and the opportunity to graduate to larger loans. The conditions and requirements for larger individual loans are more taxing than those for group lending, making these products inaccessible to women. Even clients with established businesses and credit histories struggle to obtain larger loans once they hit the ceilings established by their lending groups.

The problem of loan size is exacerbated by the up-front deduction of various fees and transaction costs, which reduces the amount available for business purposes. Most women clients start out with a small loan of about PRs 10,000 (US$111), and it takes a number of loan cycles to graduate to even moderately larger loans. Clients either have to delay the expansion of their business or borrow from more than one source. Inadequate loan size has been linked to multiple borrowing in previous research (Burki 2010) and, with the exception of clients referred by one institution, focus group discussions with field staff and clients confirm that women are borrowing from more than one source to meet their needs. Fixed fees become smaller relative to loan size as borrowers graduate to larger loans. Because women clients are often unable to obtain larger loans, however, their relative transaction costs remain higher than those of male borrowers.

Even though group-lending methodology dominates credit transactions with women, there is a clear preference for individual loans among clients, especially urban women and entrepreneurs. Seventy-five percent of focus group participants said they would prefer to borrow individually. Clients dislike being liable for someone else's loan and complained about the difficulties in forming groups (especially larger groups) and the delays that occur in disbursements due to the incomplete documentation provided by other group members.

Clients' concern about loan size seems genuine; prices and costs of doing business over the past few years have gone up but the average loan size has not (Burki 2010). But this issue may be more complex. In our discussions, 14 percent of women clients said they were content with the size of available loans. Many were clients with smaller businesses who do not have the capacity to absorb larger loans. The need is for market segmentation: increasing loan size across the board might result in exclusion of smaller borrowers, while keeping loan sizes small creates frustration and an incentive for multiple borrowing among entrepreneurs who require larger loans.

Costs of Borrowing from an MFP

In this era of high inflation, it is difficult to pay my own installment so how can I take anyone else's responsibility!

—BDS client, Lahore

Both the financial and transaction costs of borrowing from an MFP have been rising in Pakistan. Nominal interest rates on microfinance loans in Pakistan have risen in recent years and are now closer to regional benchmarks (figure 2.3). Although real interest rates remain in line internationally, as the cost in rupees rises clients conclude that the loans are expensive. In addition nearly all MFPs charge a processing fee, which varies from PRs 50 (US$0.6) to PRs 1,500 (US$17) or is expressed as a percentage (generally 1–2.5 percent) of the loan. The prevalence of bundled products, including various forms of insurance, has also increased, resulting in additional deductions and fees. Clients believe they should have the ability to opt out of these products and avoid the automatic deductions that reduce the proceeds of their loans. In some regions, clients did not even have complete information about these additional products, especially insurance products.[3]

Women entrepreneurs also bear significant transaction costs to borrow from an MFP (figure 2.4). These include the costs of fulfilling documentation requirements, and travelling and transportation expenses. Opportunity costs are incurred when women entrepreneurs are absent from their businesses for mandatory group-lending meetings, resulting in lost income. Similarly, compulsory savings, discussed later in this chapter, which often carry a penalty for withdrawal, reduce the funds available for already capital-starved businesses.

Figure 2.3 Nominal Yield on Gross Loan Portfolio, 2006–10

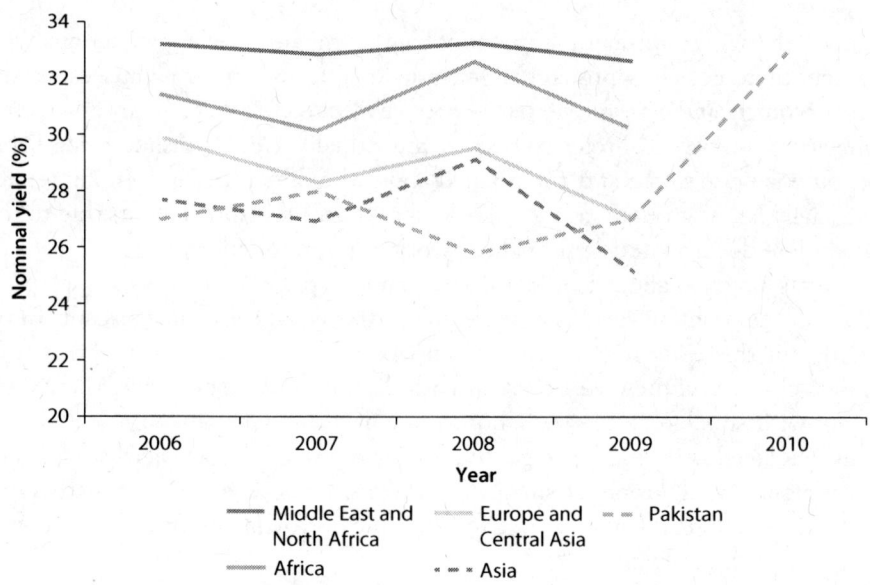

Source: Mix Market, http://www.mixmarket.org/.

Figure 2.4 Costs of a Microfinance Loan

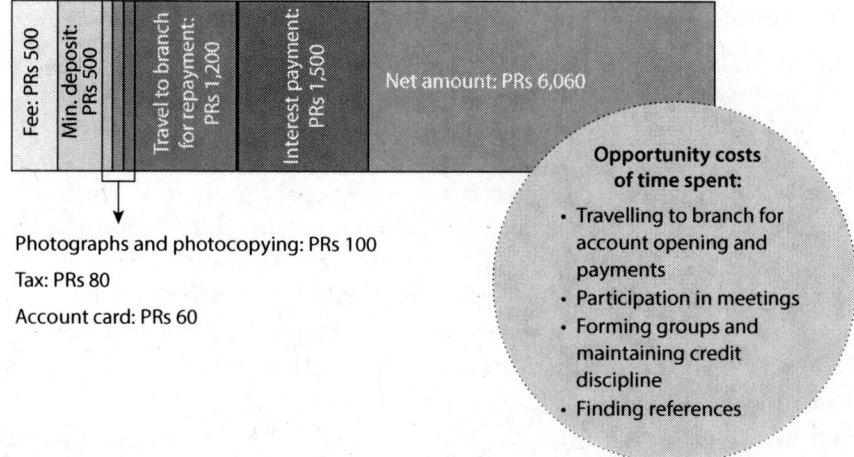

Photographs and photocopying: PRs 100

Tax: PRs 80

Account card: PRs 60

Source: Focus group discussions with clients and microfinance provider (MFP) staff and interviews with head office staff of MFPs.
Note: Figure not drawn to scale. PRs = Pakistan rupees. Exchange rate is PRs 90 = US$1.

Documentation requirements are similar across institutions. Almost all MFPs require a client's computerized national identity card along with photographs and evidence of residential status (such as a utility bill or lease). Nearly all institutions that offer individual loans require clients to provide at least two guarantors. Guarantors generally must be men, and at least one, if not both, must be unrelated to the borrower. Guarantees must take the form of legal affidavits.

Requirements such as providing a post-dated check from the guarantor's account or from a male member of the family add another layer of cost, as even men in this segment often do not have bank accounts. According to MFPs, male guarantors are necessary because it is very difficult to pursue legal action against a woman if she defaults. Although staff at some MFPs acknowledge the challenges of meeting the guarantor requirements, many discount the challenges by responding that clients understand why the guarantees are required.

Even MFPs that use the group-lending model are now requiring clients to provide personal guarantees from men. As groups become smaller, the use of guarantors mitigates risk, but at the same time creates hurdles. Respondents were quite vocal about the difficulty of meeting these requirements. Guarantors are often required to accompany the borrower to the MFP, bringing copies of the guarantor's computerized national identity card, utility bills, and other documents such as an affidavit attesting to their intent to guarantee the loan.

It is also quite common for MFPs to require the signature of a male member of the family (such as a husband, brother, or father). Some will not lend to women who cannot get a male household member's signature. The signature requirement reinforces the message that a woman requires a man's consent to take out a loan. Some MFPs require these signatures for the purpose of helping the woman—a man should share the responsibility and risk—but the message in the field is distorted and becomes "you need permission" rather than "your husband will share the responsibility." Unmarried women face even greater challenges (see box 2.2).

An Example of a Microenterprise Loan

Microfinance loan products often contain similar sets of requirements. Box 2.3 summarizes some of the most common found in loan products offered by microfinance banks (MFBs) in Pakistan.

Even in those MFBs that evolved from NGOs and have women clients with long credit histories, the percentage of women clients tends to be small or even negligible (PMN 2011). Only 24 percent of MFBs' collective clients are women compared with 81 percent for nonbank MFPs. In the National Rural Support Programme (NRSP) MFB and in the Kashf MFB, both of which evolved from

---

Box 2.2 Microfinance Lending to Unmarried Women

Requirements and attitudes within microfinance providers (MFPs) clearly lead to discrimination against single women. "[MFPs] only give to married women or [those] who [have a] guarantee of male members from family," said a BDS client. One MFP has a policy of lending only to married, widowed, or divorced women. Single women over 32 years of age are eligible, however, as they are no longer considered marriageable. This may seem absurd. From the MFP's point of view, however, lending to young, single women is highly risky: if they marry and move away, recovery of the loan becomes more complicated.

Source: Interviews with MFP staff.

Box 2.3 Product Description: Enterprise Loan of a Microfinance Bank

Requirements for an enterprise loan of PRs 10,000 (US$111) for 12 months, with equal monthly installments, in a lending group of seven; credit-life insurance included:

- Computerized national identity card, five passport-size photographs, copy of utility bill
- Should be resident of the area for at least two years
- Two years of experience in business (for new businesses, loan can be no more than PRs 5,000 [US$56] and must be repaid in six months)
- References of two persons (male or female)
- Must open a bank account with the bank, with a minimum balance of PRs 500 (US$5.5); fee for failure to maintain the minimum balance is PRs 40 (US$0.44); account closing fee is PRs 150 (US$1.7)
- Loan payments to be made at branch
- Monthly meetings at clients' homes

microfinance NGOs, women borrowers account for only 3 percent of active borrowers, compared with 72 and 100 percent for their NGOs, respectively (PMN 2011). Bank staff consider women to be the target market for their non-profit affiliates. The transformation from NGO to bank has not provided existing clients with a path to larger loans, despite the banks' being ideally positioned to make them. That said, the board of the NRSP recognizes that the imbalance needs to be addressed seriously, and efforts are already under way to develop products for women in both credit and savings. As the bank rolls out its products, we can expect to see these ratios improve. NRSP Bank has a rural focus, however, and lending for agriculture remains its main product; agriculture is not a sector dominated by women. Kashf MFB may also improve its outreach to women as it stabilizes and recovers from the 2008 delinquency crisis, which seriously impaired both its nonprofit arm and its portfolio.

Discussions with field staff revealed that women's businesses are often perceived as small-scale setups instead of "enterprises," thus making them invisible as a market to institutions engaged in making larger loans. In one MFP, for example, enterprise loans were marketed only in marketplaces, where few women entrepreneurs were located, and even the women loan officers dealing with female groups were unaware that those loans were available.

Findings from Focus Group Discussions: Savings

Although MFPs, especially MFBs, are trying to attract savings in the informal, nonbank sector, there are few success stories. Even products that were designed to attract women have not achieved any significant success. Women continue to save at home and in lending groups. Half the sample was saving in lending groups, and 40 percent used other means such as keeping cash at home, with friends,

Figure 2.5 Trends in Saving in Pakistan, 2003–10

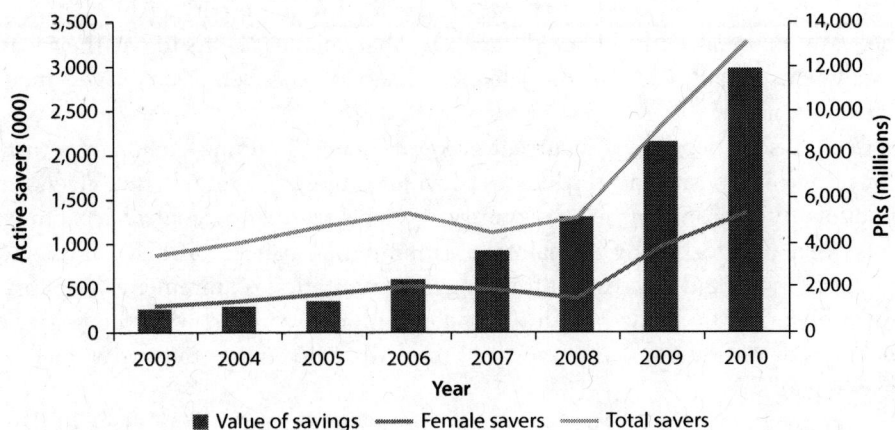

Source: Pakistan Microfinance Network, http://www.microfinancepakistan.com.
Note: PRs = Pakistan rupees. Exchange rate is PRs 90 = US$1.

or with relatives. Although 36 percent of the women in our sample had bank accounts, few used them regularly.[4]

Savings have been steadily increasing, however, since 2008 (see figure 2.5). Most of the savers live in rural areas owing to the extensive effort to attract savings carried out by the National Rural Support Programme, which alone accounts for 60 percent of the total female savers and 62 percent of total rural savers. Urban savers are mostly MFB clients and generally men; only 31 percent of urban savers are women.

In order to accommodate both small savers and large deposits, the range of savings products offered by MFBs is larger and more diverse than that of microfinance institutions (MFIs). MFB products resemble those of commercial banks with easier terms and conditions to suit the relevant target markets. Nearly all banks offer current and savings accounts, and some offer term certificates. Some MFPs have experimented with the use of committees to capture informal savings. In case of MFIs, savings are often a compulsory component of borrowing, and borrowers are required to regularly contribute a minimum amount (between PRs 50 [US$0.55] and PRs 300 [US$3.33] per month) toward their savings.

Branchless banking may represent one of the most exciting opportunities for expanding women's access to financial services in Pakistan. The Consultative Group to Assist the Poor (2011) cites Pakistan as one of the fastest developing markets for branchless banking in the world and a "laboratory for innovation." Developments in the sector have come about rapidly in the wake of the State Bank of Pakistan's 2009 *Branchless Banking Regulations*, which allow the use of agent networks and mobile devices as distribution channels for financial products and services by the banking sector. The study's findings indicate that women's access to mobile phones is quite high. In urban areas, especially larger cities like Lahore, over 60 percent of clients have their own phones; nearly all others have access to a phone owned by a family member. In rural areas, ownership drops to between 30 and 40 percent, but access to a family-owned phone is still quite high. Those who had used *easypaisa* or *Omni* (through a partnership between the Kashf Foundation and United Bank Ltd. that enables clients to pay their loan installments at any Omni outlet) liked the service and believed it saved them time and money.

Compulsory deposits and current accounts generally do not yield any return. Longer-term deposits and certificates provide competitive returns but, given the inflationary environment in the country, are unattractive to clients. Savers must often bear fees for failing to maintain a minimum balance, for ATM cards, and for checkbooks, and the costs of fulfilling documentation requirements. The costs of travelling to the branch, both of time and money, coupled with the negative real rates of return and deductions for taxes create little incentive for women to save in banks.

Compulsory saving creates additional issues—women dislike the lack of flexibility and lack of access to their money. Clients reinforce the observations of staff and say that the returns just do not outweigh the costs of keeping small savings in a bank. They also worry that their funds would not be available for an emergency after banking hours. A number of business development service respondents were reluctant as they lacked information and knowledge about banks and formal saving mechanisms. MFP staff often cited confidentiality as one of the reasons that women want to save in banks; women often have to be accompanied by a family member (often male) when they travel to a bank branch, however, compromising their confidentiality.

Most women who have bank accounts gave positive feedback regarding bank staff and account opening processes. These clients found ATMs quite useful and did not find documentation requirements difficult. They also believe that by placing money in the bank they "put it out of the way of temptation" and cannot spend it as readily as they might were it available as ready cash at home.

Most women entrepreneurs seem fully aware of their options for formal and informal saving. Many of them choose to combine various saving mechanisms to meet different financial needs. They recognize the advantages of saving both formally and informally (see table 2.1). Their preference to save informally is

Table 2.1 Advantages of Formal and Informal Saving

Advantages of saving formally (banks, post offices, MFPs)	Advantages of saving informally (at home, through savings groups, with neighbors)
• Security: savings kept in a bank are secure from theft	• Flexibility: control of amount to be saved
• Confidentiality: information about personal savings can be kept confidential from neighbors, relatives, and even husbands	• Easy access: money is available at all times if kept at home or with neighbors
• Financial discipline: cash at home can be spent— putting it in a bank creates financial discipline	• Savings discipline: savings groups require forced savings, enabling clients to save significant amounts
• Certainty: savings groups sometimes break down but savings products of banks are consistent	• Convenient: do not need to travel, saving time and money
	• Low cost: no fees or charges

Source: Focus group discussions with microfinance provider (MFP) clients.

based largely on a cost-benefit analysis rather than on lack of information, difficult procedures, or attitudes of staff.

Findings from Focus Group Discussions: Insurance

If they're not going to give [benefits], why do they deduct our money?

—NRSP client, Rajanpur

Most MFPs have partnered with mainstream insurance companies to offer insurance products, especially health insurance, to their clients. Some institutions have chosen to offer credit-life insurance directly to avoid the additional costs of such partnerships that would have to be passed on to the client without any additional benefit. Box 2.4 lists the common features of credit-life and health insurance offered by MFPs.

There is a considerable divergence of views between the head office and field staffs about insurance. Almost universally, senior management of MFPs believe that these products are very popular among clients and provide them with significant benefits and security. Documentation requirements and payment processes were believed to be efficient, and the claims-payment ratio reasonably high. Feedback from field staff and clients was less positive. In the case of health insurance, field staff and clients both believed that documentation requirements and conditions for filing claims were onerous and complex and that "clients get

---

Box 2.4 Insurance Product Features

Credit-Life Insurance

- Outstanding loans are paid off in the event of the policyholder's death or, in some cases, permanent disability.
- A payout of between PRs 3,000 (US$33) and PRs 5,000 (US$56) is made to the policyholder's family for funeral expenses. In a few cases the amount is quite small (PRs 1,500 [US$17]) or relatively large (PRs 15,000 [US$167]).
- Annual premiums are either a flat rate between PRs 150 (US$1.7) and PRs 250 (US$2.8) per person or a percentage (generally 1–2 percent) of the loan amount.
- The product is nearly always bundled with a credit product and is compulsory.

Health Insurance

- Generally both the client and the spouse are covered.
- Per annum coverage varies from PRs 10,000 (US$111) to PRs 50,000 (US$556) and is generally limited to hospitalization costs.
- Premiums, paid on varying schedules, range from PRs 100 (US$1.1) for minimal coverage and from PRs 250 (US$2.8) to PRs 480 (US$5.3) for products offering greater coverage.
- The product is nearly always bundled with a credit product and is compulsory.

Source: Interviews and focus group discussions with microfinance provider staff.

---

fed up after a while." According to an NRSP credit officer in Bahawalpur, only 1–2 percent of clients file claims for reimbursement, and payout can take six to eight months. Out of those who do manage to file claims, the wider perception is that insurance providers do not pay.[5]

A number of respondents either did not know they had paid for insurance or did not understand what purchasing insurance meant. In some cases clients knew their loan would be paid off under the credit-life product if they died, but did not know that funeral expenses would also be provided.

Clients must be made aware of insurance and its benefits. Equally important, however, clients must understand the conditions under which payments will be made to policyholders. A number of respondents cited examples of people they knew who had insurance, but received no money. In other cases, the reimbursement took such a long time that it was of no use to the clients. These incidents have created an air of mistrust toward insurance products in the market. Although the majority of MFP field staff believe that clients understand the concept of insurance, the results of the focus group discussions indicate that clients require greater transparency and clearer information. Staff might not be spending sufficient time explaining these products because they are bundled with credit products and not marketed separately. The sale of insurance products has no effect on the staff's targets and incentives.

The absence of a wide network of health infrastructure, especially in rural areas, means clients often have to travel, at significant cost, to nearby towns and cities for checkups and treatment. Most health insurance products operate on a reimbursement system, that is, the client pays for treatment herself and can then claim reimbursement upon submission of required documentation. As an NRSP client from Bahawalpur put it, "A poor person will not have money to get treatment in the first place, thus will not file a claim and the organization doesn't have to pay!" Uncertainty about whether the claim will be paid, the time and money required to provide the requisite documentation, and low levels of coverage discourage clients, and it is doubtful that many would be interested in these products were they optional instead of compulsory.

Another source of insurance is State Life Insurance, a public sector insurance company incorporated in 1972, which is the largest provider of life insurance in Pakistan. Its products seem to be popular in this market segment. Some clients had taken out education policies for their sons and life insurance policies for themselves and their spouses. Clients use these products as long-term savings vehicles, contributing anywhere from PRs 2,000 (US$22) to PRs 10,000 (US$111) annually in exchange for a lump-sum payment after 15–20 years. Clients are happy with these life insurance products, which benefit them during their lifetime while also mitigating financial risk. Reactions to credit-life insurance were mixed, however; although some clients were satisfied that their loan would be paid off in the event of their death and that their family would not be burdened, a number of respondents were troubled that there would be no significant benefit to them during their lifetime and by the limited coverage for funeral expenses.

Notes

1. For example, marketing strategies of MFPs show that information about larger loans is disseminated in the marketplace rather than within groups. Most women do not operate in the marketplace and are not aware of such products. Also, women are expected to "graduate" to larger, individual loans even if they have a running business, unlike men, whose first loans can be individual loans.

2. This definition has been adopted by some institutions, such as the Small and Medium Enterprise Development Authority in Pakistan, that work on entrepreneurship development.

3. For example, one out of five clients of Tameer MFB in Rawalpindi did not know she was paying for insurance as a bundled product; women in a focus group in Rawalpindi with Akhuwat lending-group clients knew that the loan would be paid in the event of the borrower's death but did not know there was a death benefit payment of PRs 5,000 (US$56); National Rural Support Programme (NRSP) clients in Dera Ghazi (DG) Khan had no knowledge of bundled insurance; and one BDS client in Quetta commented that Khushhali Bank Ltd. charges for insurance but does not inform clients.

4. Because most women use multiple modes of saving, totals add up to more than 100 percent.

5. For example, an NRSP staff member in DG Khan said that, out of 850 clients, 4 or 5 filed claims, of which 2 were rejected and 2 received some payment; another staff member had 525 clients filing 20–25 claims with only 5–7 receiving payment. In Rajanpur, a client said, "[Through] NRSP insurance, no one ever got money." One client said that after her husband's death, NRSP did not provide funeral expenses and still required repayment of the loan. Some business development service clients in Sukkur had concerns about the reliability of insurance as they had heard of cases in which the insured's family was not given any payment after his or her death.

References

Burki, Hussan-Bano. 2010. *Microcredit Utilization: Shifting from Production to Consumption.* Islamabad: Pakistan Microfinance Network.

CGAP (Consultative Group to Assist the Poor). 2011. *Branchless Banking in Pakistan: A Laboratory for Innovation.* Washington, DC: CGAP.

PMN (Pakistan Microfinance Network). 2011. *MicroWATCH* 22 (October–December). http://www.scribd.com/doc/86644843/Micro-Watch-Issue-22.

CHAPTER 3

Do Women Benefit from an Enabling Policy Environment for Microfinance?

Pakistan is recognized as a global leader in the development of progressive and innovative policies to promote financial access for women. Most important has been the deliberate effort to ensure that the development finance agenda is carried out by the private sector under the regulatory supervision of the State Bank of Pakistan (SBP). The Pakistan Poverty Alleviation Fund (PPAF) provides financing and supports the development of institutions that can make financial access available on a permanent basis to those at the bottom of Pakistan's economic ladder. Pakistan is also at the forefront of innovation in branchless banking—an example of how the right policy framework fosters experimentation.

The policy and strategic framework for microfinance is gender neutral—it neither limits access to credit or finance for women nor places special emphasis on increasing outreach. Outreach to women has grown mostly through institutions that, by virtue of their own mission, choose to target women. The level of outreach to women borrowers and entrepreneurs has been measured and monitored based on the number of women clients; that indicator can be misleading, however, because a large percentage of these loans is used by another household member, not the nominal female borrower.

Pakistan's broader poverty alleviation strategies, as defined in the two *Poverty Reduction Strategy Papers*, provide a framework under which different policies of the government related to, among other things, health, education, and inclusion of women are developed. These strategies recognize that women in Pakistan are marginalized and more vulnerable than men, that female poverty is acute, and that Pakistan lags in female literacy. Microfinance's benefits to women are also acknowledged and reiterated. A commitment is made to increase the outreach of credit services, especially for women, and to include monitoring mechanisms to review progress related to women's access to finance. The government's latest strategy on economic growth[1] recognizes the need to facilitate female entrepreneurship, especially among young women in urban areas, through reducing the costs of setting up small and micro businesses, and the need to create equal opportunities for men and women.

At a practical level, microfinance policy frameworks have had greater influence in shaping the priorities of the sector. These include *Microfinance Institution Ordinance 2001* (State Bank of Pakistan 2001), *Expanding Microfinance Outreach Strategy* (State Bank of Pakistan 2007), and the *Strategic Framework for Sustainable Microfinance in Pakistan* (State Bank of Pakistan 2011b). Each was developed under the leadership of the SBP, which is generally viewed as a driver of policy on microfinance. The SBP encourages market-based mechanisms and focuses on creating an environment that promotes inclusive finance on a sustainable basis; its strategic policy frameworks emphasize the provision of appropriate and affordable financial services for all, including women. The three policy frameworks are summarized below.

- *Microfinance Institution Ordinance 2001* purports to promote microfinance as a private sector initiative, regulated by the SBP, for the purpose of poverty reduction, particularly for women. There is very little focus on women, however, beyond that generalization. In the initial phases of supporting the sector, the challenge was to develop successful business models. Guidance on mechanisms for institutionalizing increased access to finance for women and developing policies that will promote gender sensitivity in the sector and at the institutional level is missing.

- *Expanding Microfinance Outreach Strategy* (2007) focused on growth and identified the need to promote microfinance in rural areas and to women. It also sought to develop monitoring mechanisms to oversee the social impact of microfinance by requiring disaggregated data for rural, urban, and women's access to finance. No gender-disaggregated targets were set, however, and no special incentives or means of recognizing organizations that succeed in serving women well were included in the final document.

- *Strategic Framework for Sustainable Microfinance in Pakistan* (2011) is based on "promoting market-based financial services that meet the diverse needs of poor and low-income segments." It focuses on quality of growth, product diversification, financial inclusion, corporate governance, management professionalization, and sector-level infrastructure to avoid client risk through the establishment of credit bureau, consumer protection, and financial literacy initiatives. The underlying premise is that establishment of strong and sustainable microfinance providers (MFPs), with a focus on niche markets and oversight by regulators, will lead to growth, improved quality of services, consumer protection and literacy, and focus on the core mission of access to finance, especially in rural markets and by women. A clear matrix is provided to indicate disaggregated data on access to finance by women and in rural areas.

These policy frameworks provide strategic direction to sector stakeholders, including MFPs, donors, funders, associations, supervisors, and others. Prudential regulations provide a legal framework by which all microfinance banks (MFBs) are bound. Two sets of regulations govern microfinance banking operations in Pakistan: the *Prudential Regulations for Microfinance Banks* (State Bank of Pakistan 2011a) and the *Branchless Banking Regulations* (State Bank of Pakistan 2011c).

The *Prudential Regulations for Microfinance Banks* have recently been updated by the SBP. The regulations specifically promote the financial soundness of MFBs, but also focus on increasing access to marginalized segments of potential borrowers. For example, Prudential Regulation 17 (prevention of criminal use of MFB channels for the purposes of money laundering and other unlawful trade) allows MFBs to extend microcredit in remote areas to borrowers, particularly women, who do not have computerized national identity cards (CNICs), passports, or driver's licenses. Prudential Regulation 3 promotes "adequate female representation on [boards of directors]" (State Bank of Pakistan 2011a, 20).

The *Branchless Banking Regulations* were promulgated by the SBP in March 2008. The purposes of branchless banking are promotion of growth and improved efficiency in the financial sector. The regulations do not specifically limit access to financial services by women. The know-your-customer requirement that makes possession of a CNIC compulsory may be viewed by some as a barrier to women (far fewer women than men have CNICs[2]), but many sector stakeholders, including the Pakistan Microfinance Network (PMN), believe promotion of the use of CNICs to be in the larger national interest at both the micro and macro levels. The CNIC is a requirement for nearly all legal and business transactions in Pakistan. The National Database and Registration Authority and MFPs must work together (through, for example, the PMN) to ensure that acquisition of CNICs is made easier for potential clients of financial services, especially women. Branchless banking models generally involve the use of mobile phones; the development of a set of gender-disaggregated data by the Pakistan Telecommunication Authority could facilitate financial access for women through branchless banking platforms.

There are similar concerns that the recent launch of the Microfinance Credit Information Bureau in Pakistan, use of which requires a CNIC, might result in a failure to increase or even a reduction in financial access for women. Data obtained from MFPs show, however, that a large number of clients already possess a CNIC, and the research for this study found that many acquire one in order to apply for loans.

The SBP currently manages one of the largest donor funds for microfinance in Pakistan—the £50 million Financial Inclusion Program of the Department for International Development-UK (DFID). The SBP is using this program to focus on female clients and has set targets for grantee institutions for increasing access to women. Funding requests by MFPs with an exclusive focus on women are given priority. Once the grants are approved, gender and youth indicators are assigned with outreach targets for implementation during the project life and regularly monitored during the course of the project.

Multilateral and bilateral donors have consistently supported the implementation of the government's and SBP's strategies for microfinance. Some of the key milestones in the sector's development were achieved through donor assistance. Donors continue to see microfinance as an effective tool for economic empowerment but find that lack of effective institutions and capacity constraints limit the growth of microfinance. Additional challenges include (1) social taboos related to women's roles and expectations; (2) low literacy levels; (3) lack of access to capital, markets, and information; (4) women's limited mobility and weak skill base; and (5) lack of customized financial products for women entrepreneurs. Many donors in Pakistan remain committed to addressing women's issues, including livelihoods and access to finance, with the DFID and Canadian International Development Agency (CIDA) expressing the greatest interest in microfinance.[3]

As the single largest source of funds for nonbank MFPs, PPAF exerts a strong influence on the practice of microfinance in Pakistan. It has focused, as have other policy institutions, mainly on outreach numbers of clients when looking at issues of women's access to finance. A recent change in management appears to have led to a greater commitment to dealing with this challenge, and PPAF is working to incorporate gender awareness into its programs as well as into its own operations. Explicit targets for outreach have been given to its partners, which will be monitored closely. PPAF has pledged to eliminate product features and policies that discriminate against women. Funding was provided to microfinance institutions to test women-focused products, which has resulted in several successful projects (see box 3.1). The challenge now is expanding these products to serve more clients.

The PMN, the national association for MFPs, has also been actively involved in shaping the microfinance landscape. It has successfully advocated for a shift toward sustainable practices and worked closely with policy makers to provide strategic direction and improve the capacity of service providers. It has played only a limited role, however, in highlighting the issue of women's access to finance.

The government and donors place considerable emphasis on women's access to finance in their strategies and policies. But an important finding from this study relates to the types of outcomes that are expected and measured. Nearly all reporting and monitoring revolve around the number of active women clients. This indicator, although important, is usually misleading and incomplete. Prior evidence and the research for this study show that a large proportion of loans to women are passed on to men—husbands, fathers, brothers, and sons. Thus, even though existing policies do not seem to prohibit or even discourage outreach to women, progress on this agenda in Pakistan will require a more visible push rather than the neutral stance of the current policy environment. Economic pressures and the changing sociocultural dynamics of Pakistan are already pushing more and more women into the workforce, including as entrepreneurs. Initiatives like the SBP's Nationwide Financial Literacy Program are important in raising

Box 3.1 Funding Innovation for Women-Focused Financial Products

The Pakistan Poverty Alleviation Fund (PPAF) supported a number of pilot projects under its Microfinance Innovation & Outreach Programme, funded by the International Fund for Agricultural Development. At least six of these were focused solely on women. Experiments with longer loan terms, larger loans, varied repayment schedules, cluster-based lending, and asset transfers were supported. Successful projects included:

• Women's Livestock Cooperative Farming: This project, which focused on poor rural women, integrated group lending and cooperative farming and created links with market and government departments. Group loans were made and the proceeds used to purchase and fatten goats on a commercial basis. Technical support was provided by a livestock dairy board and other technical experts. The project targeted poor women who did not qualify for microfinance. Repayment schedules varied to match the cash flow from sales of livestock.

• Community Investment Fund (CIF) Project: A community investment fund is owned and managed by community institutions that target the poorest, especially the poorest women members. Under this project a community investment fund is created through a contribution from the National Rural Support Programme and PPAF. Approximately 70 percent of the funds are used for onlending to the institutions' members and the rest is used to cover operational expenses. The revolving credit pool and the income it generates enable the institution to attain financial and operational self-sufficiency.

• Strengthening Microenterprises Project: Recognizing the needs of women who run microenterprises, this project integrated skills and vocational training, creation of upstream and downstream market links, and provision of financial services. The project uses a three-pronged strategy: financial resources for onlending, technical assistance in the form of business development services, and links to markets. Using a cluster-based approach, women were supported in businesses such as hosiery, furniture, and ceramics. Loans were larger than otherwise available (from PRs 150,000 [US$1,667] to PRs 200,000 [US$2,222]), loan terms were longer, and loans were made on an individual basis.

Source: Discussions with staff of the Pakistan Poverty Alleviation Fund.

the understanding of target populations, including women, in managing household resources and enterprise financing. There is a tremendous opportunity in this changing scenario, but one that requires additional commitment from all stakeholders, including policy makers.

Notes

1. Planning Commission, Government of Pakistan, "Framework for Economic Growth—Pakistan 2011," http://www.pc.gov.pk/hot%20links/growth_document_english_version.pdf.

2. Dawn.com, http://dawn.com/2012/08/18/96pc-adults-registered-in-pakistan-nadra-2/.

3. Based on discussions with donors including United Nations Development Programme, CIDA, International Finance Corporation, European Commission, U.S. Agency for International Development, and DFID. See appendix C.

References

State Bank of Pakistan. 2001. *Microfinance Institution Ordinance 2001*. Karachi, Pakistan.

———. 2007. *Expanding Microfinance Outreach Strategy*. Karachi, Pakistan.

———. 2011a. *Prudential Regulations for Microfinance Banks*. Karachi, Pakistan.

———. 2011b. *Strategic Framework for Sustainable Microfinance in Pakistan*. Karachi, Pakistan.

———. 2011c. *Branchless Banking Regulations for Financial Institutions Desirous to Undertake Branchless Banking*. Karachi, Pakistan.

CHAPTER 4

Conclusion and Recommendations for Stakeholders

Behind the overall numbers of micro-credit accounts and million dollar portfolios we may find, not growing numbers of happy enterprising women and men working their way out of poverty, but, on the contrary, evidence for mission drift, irresponsible lending and more obvious benefits to the MFI and its investors than to intended clients.

—Rhyne 2010

Although microfinance outreach to female borrowers has increased in recent years, using the number of women clients alone as an indicator of women's financial inclusion can be misleading. This study shows that a high percentage of the loans taken by women are likely passed on to male family members. Despite an enabling environment and strong policy framework, women entrepreneurs in Pakistan remain financially excluded and continue to rely on informal sources of credit. Very few of the financial services offered by microfinance institutions are suitable for these women. Other microfinance services, such as savings and insurance products, are compulsory and bundled with credit products; therefore, their value cannot be separately assessed. Although based on qualitative data, the findings suggest that much more can be done to ensure that outreach is inclusive.

An increase in the financial inclusion of women, and more focus on women entrepreneurship, will require a strong "push" from donors, the State Bank of Pakistan (SBP), the Pakistan Poverty Alleviation Fund (PPAF), and the Pakistan Microfinance Network (PMN). The policy and funding environment strongly affects the operation of microfinance providers (MFPs); in the absence of pressure from policy makers and donors, most MFPs have little or no incentive to focus on the issues of women. A shift in donor emphasis is necessary and contingent on a change in the approach to microfinance. The notion of the sustainability of MFPs must be expanded to include the sustainability of their clients' businesses, and the emphasis on rapid growth must become an emphasis on responsible and inclusive growth. Only then will donors give women's inclusion the priority and consistent attention that will signal change to MFPs. MFPs, in turn, must understand that women's inclusion is integral to the objectives of microfinance. The boards of directors of MFPs, entrusted with the guardianship of their missions, will have to play an active role and take responsibility for carrying out their avowed objective of women's economic empowerment. They need to create innovative solutions that challenge patriarchal assumptions, not reinforce them.

Today, there are signs of a shift in emphasis in the world of microfinance. At the international level, crises in microfinance have led to a greater awareness of the need to look beyond numbers, to focus on the quality of microfinance services, and to ensure that the poor, particularly women, are beneficiaries and not victims of microfinance. The work of the Social Performance Task Force, the Smart Campaign, Microfinance Transparency, Women's World Banking, and the Women's Empowerment Mainstreaming and Networking's efforts to develop a seal of excellence and indicators to assess gender equity are evidence of a greater focus on client protection, ethical financial practices, pricing transparency, social performance management, and delivering on the promise of women's empowerment (Sinha 2011).

In this new scenario, microfinance stakeholders will face new challenges. Can women who bear the transaction costs but pass the loan on to another person be reported as clients? Are they to be considered "financially included"? What accounts for the low usage rates of loans and savings products by women? Why lend through women if men are using a large percentage of the loans? Are the products offered meeting women's needs as entrepreneurs and financial managers? Is the group-lending methodology empowering or disempowering? If women entrepreneurs have a clear and strong preference for individual lending, why is their access to individual loans so limited? What needs to be done to facilitate women's economic empowerment?

Changes in the world of microfinance have begun to influence donor policies and funding in Pakistan as well. Incidents of delinquency seen since 2008 have also led some MFPs to review their procedures and policies. In some cases, women's demands for one meeting a month and smaller groups have now been met. The PPAF, which has a strong commitment to women's empowerment, functions as the principal donor for MFPs and, since 2011, under its new management, as a quasi-regulator. MFPs now have an opportunity to develop services and products women value, thus increasing women's use of financial services, which is integral to MFPs' achieving their financial and social objectives.

This chapter provides concrete suggestions for key stakeholders in the sector, such as the SBP, PMN, and PPAF, and guidelines to help MFPs develop products and services with features valued by women. There is much that can be done by each stakeholder, and donors can support key stakeholders in the design and implementation of customized solutions (box 4.1).

Box 4.1 High-Priority Recommendations for Microfinance Sector Stakeholders in Pakistan

- The State Bank of Pakistan (SBP) and the Pakistan Poverty Alleviation Fund (PPAF) should make clear that using women as conduits for loans to men is a serious consumer protection issue and that tracking and monitoring of loan use must be transparent and realistic. The tracking of gender-disaggregated loan utilization data could be required and monitored through existing supervision and monitoring systems. Alternatively, less costly risk-based mechanisms, including periodic audits, could be used to ensure compliance.
- SBP and PPAF should also require that loan application processes not discriminate against women through, for example, exclusive reliance on male guarantors or exclusion of unmarried women. A description of the terms and conditions of each product that is offered by an MFP, according to a specified format, would make the loan application process transparent. This will also help to ensure that there are no criteria that discriminate by gender.
- Microfinance providers (MFPs) should design pilot projects for women entrepreneurs by incorporating valued features identified in this study, such as larger, individual loans with flexible installments, longer repayment periods, and less restrictive guarantor requirements.
- The Pakistan Microfinance Network (PMN) should promote partnerships within its membership to expand innovations in branchless banking and explore potential alliances with telecommunications companies and postal networks.
- PMN can ensure a sustained focus on women's inclusion in microfinance through lectures, seminars, a yearly micro-note publication, and the incorporation of gender as a criterion in its data collection, research, policy dialogues, consumer protection efforts, and benchmarks on financial and social performance.
- MFPs should collect gender-disaggregated data on loan utilization with the purpose of reporting transparently on clients and using the data in strategic planning to increase women's utilization of loans.

State Bank of Pakistan

The SBP currently regulates more than half the microfinance service providers registered under the *Microfinance Institution Ordinance 2001* (State Bank of Pakistan 2001). As the leading driver of vision and policy for the microfinance sector, the SBP has the ability to create a more positive environment for expanding women's access to and use of financial services.

Strong directives through policy frameworks and supporting prudential regulations for women's inclusion will influence the policies and practices of microfinance banks (MFBs). The SBP can play an important role in promoting the understanding that women's inclusion in financial services is not simply about the number of women clients but about MFBs (1) ensuring their processes do not discriminate against women and (2) creating products and services that enhance opportunities for women, especially women entrepreneurs. The gender dimensions of customer satisfaction, consumer protection, and social performance need to be highlighted. Incentives for MFPs that can provide evidence of such products and services need to be considered. Regulations may be further strengthened to include specific regulations that promote women's inclusion and can be monitored. The following are suggested:

- The *Strategic Framework for Sustainable Microfinance in Pakistan* (State Bank of Pakistan 2011) should be revised to include an explicit emphasis on the financial inclusion of women, using the resources and documents of Department for International Development-UK's *Financial Inclusion Program* as a guide. In addition, the 2011 framework should also promote strong corporate governance and direct boards of MFPs, as guardians of their mission, to ensure that the objectives of women's economic inclusion and empowerment are translated into practice. The SBP could ensure gender diversity on boards by specifying that a minimum percentage of directors should be women.[1]

- Existing prudential regulations and know-your-customer requirements cannot be implemented effectively if the actual user of a loan is different from the nominal borrower, as is the case when a woman is used as a conduit. The SBP should specify that the use of women as conduits for loans to men is an unacceptable practice from the perspectives of prudence and ethics. The SBP should require that loan-use data be tracked and reported by MFBs and verified by the SBP's inspection process. Alternatively, less costly risk-based mechanisms, including periodic audits, could be used to ensure compliance. The SBP should also require that the loan application process not discriminate against women by requiring the signature of her spouse, requiring an additional guarantor, or accepting only male guarantors for loans. Compliance with these regulations could be monitored by the SBP's inspection teams.

- A description of the terms and conditions of each product that is offered by an MFP, according to a specified format, would make the loan application process transparent. MFPs should be required to make these descriptions available to all clients and ensure that they are read and understood. This will also help to eliminate criteria that discriminate by gender.

Pakistan Microfinance Network

PMN plays a key role in the sector. It serves as an information hub for the industry through data collection and analysis, research and publications, organizing events and policy roundtables, and promoting benchmarks on financial and social performance. It works closely with policy makers, donors, and regulators, building strategic partnerships with local and international stakeholders. PMN also builds the capacity of the sector through local and international training, exposure visits, and links with academic institutions. The PMN should actively promote a focus on women's financial inclusion in all its undertakings. Some recommendations are:

- Ensure a sustained focus on women's inclusion in microfinance through lectures, seminars, a yearly micro-note publication, and the incorporation of gender as a criterion in its data collection, research, policy dialogues, consumer protection efforts, and benchmarks on financial and social performance.
- Use its pivotal role in the setting of policy to address women's financial issues in SBP and donor policies.
- Build capacity and provide technical assistance in the development of products and services to promote the financial inclusion of women and women entrepreneurs.
- Conduct research on a regular basis to assess the level of financial inclusion of women entrepreneurs.
- Develop a format for product descriptions for regulated and unregulated MFPs.
- Promote partnerships within its membership to expand innovations in branchless banking and explore potential alliances with telecommunications companies and postal networks. Create a database on women's financial inclusion that can be accessed by MFPs.
- Use surveys on financial literacy and usage to develop an evidenced-based approach to understanding the financial needs of households.

Pakistan Poverty Alleviation Fund

PPAF, an apex institution, has played a central role in the growth of the microfinance sector in Pakistan, both in increasing the number of MFPs and in client outreach. Although initially created as an apex fund for onlending by the World Bank, PPAF has played a much broader role in microfinance by supporting its partner organizations through institutional strengthening, capacity building, exposure to best practices, and linking with commercial funding sources. Despite the recent diversification in the sector, nonregulated MFPs continue to rely heavily on PPAF for funding, and in the absence of a sectorwide regulatory framework, PPAF has emerged as a quasi-regulator for nonbank MFPs. It exerts a strong influence on the policies and strategies of its partner organizations and is well positioned to play an important role in encouraging MFPs to promote women's financial inclusion. Some recommendations are:

- Develop funding criteria that give priority to organizations that have created products valued and used by women and that have promoted gender diversity on their staffs and boards. An award could be given to organizations that have been successful in enhancing economic opportunities for women.

- Specify that, within a given time period, partners should have a minimum percentage of women on their boards, including one member who has an in-depth knowledge of gender issues in Pakistan. These women should be trained to ensure they are able to fully participate in all board activities.
- Specify that the use of women as conduits for loans to men is an unacceptable practice from the perspectives of prudence and ethics and require that gender-disaggregated loan-use data be tracked and reported by MFP partners and verified by PPAF.
- Adopt a zero-tolerance policy for loan application processes that discriminate against women by requiring the signature of her spouse, requiring an additional guarantor for women, or accepting only male guarantors for loans. Compliance could be monitored by PPAF's inspection teams.
- A description of the terms and conditions of each product that is offered by an MFP, according to a specified format, would make the loan application process transparent. MFPs should be required to make these descriptions available to all clients and ensure that they are read and understood. This will also help to eliminate criteria that discriminate by gender.
- Encourage partners that lend only to women to lend directly to men, so women do not have to bear the transaction costs of loans they do not use.
- Support pilot projects that test the potential of reaching women through branchless banking for a range of financial services, especially savings.
- Host national and international conferences on women's financial inclusion.
- Provide technical assistance to partners to develop products and processes that result in greater financial inclusion of women and support expansion of successful pilot projects.
- Document and disseminate success stories from existing and pilot projects.

Microfinance Providers

MFPs in Pakistan include regulated MFPs, rural support programs offering microfinance and other programs, and specialized as well as broad-range nongovernmental organizations. Microfinance is intended to provide financial services to the poor; because women constitute half the population, and a disproportionate percentage of the poor, the entire range of MFPs is accountable for women's financial inclusion. Based on the research conducted, this study recommends concrete steps MFPs can take to ensure that women are not being discriminated against and that there are products and services that meet their specific needs as entrepreneurs. MFPs should:

- Commit senior management to creating and promoting products and services that meet the demands of women entrepreneurs.
- Ensure that none of the loan application processes discriminate against women.
- Promote gender diversity at different levels of staff in the organization and on the board.

- Collect gender-disaggregated data on loan use to enable transparent reporting of clients and use the data in strategic planning to increase women's use of loans.
- Develop a comprehensive description of products according to a standardized format and share it with female and male clients to ensure transparency and informed choice.
- Design pilot projects for women entrepreneurs by incorporating the following valued features:
  - Larger loan sizes (PRs 50,000 [US$556] to PRs 150,000 [US$1,667])
  - Longer repayment periods (18–24 months)
  - Flexible installments (and grace periods, if applicable) based on cash flows of specific businesses
  - Individual or small groups (two to five borrowers) of variable size
  - Guarantor requirements that allow women entrepreneurs to guarantee each other's loans
- Allow prepayment of loans.
- Design products for women working in a specific business cluster by tailoring the loan amount, size of installments, and repayment period to the cash flows of that business.
- Develop links with business development service providers and use their criteria to locate strong women entrepreneurs who might be potential clients.
- Test the potential for branchless banking to offer a range of financial services to women.

Our research shows that designing a pilot project does not involve simply designing a product; the processes associated with the delivery of the product have to be systematically and periodically analyzed and fine-tuned. The product and its delivery mechanisms have to be aligned and embedded in the overall strategy of the MFP, and all the staff involved have to be trained to understand its objectives and methodology. Staff incentives must be aligned with the new product, and training programs for analysis of creditworthiness must be developed. Gender-sensitive marketing strategies that are designed to attract women entrepreneurs may differ substantially from the strategies used for men. MFPs should also consider assigning a dedicated employee to oversee and champion the entire process.

Conclusion

Pakistan's microfinance sector has a strong track record of global leadership in fostering innovations in service delivery, demonstrating resiliency in the face of crises, and developing progressive regulatory and policy standards. Addressing the challenges of gender raised by this report presents another opportunity to demonstrate global policy leadership and the ability to innovate in providing financial services to women. The challenges of consumer protection and effectively reaching women entrepreneurs are likely not limited to Pakistan. By moving aggressively and pragmatically to tackle these issues, Pakistan will once again demonstrate its position as a global leader, pushing outward the frontier of financial outreach to women, and as a model for other countries in the region and around the world.

Note

1. Various countries, especially in Europe, are moving toward imposing quotas ranging from 20 to 40 percent for the representation of women on corporate boards (Heidrick & Struggles 2010). A number of studies (mainly in developed countries) have been published that examine gender diversity on boards and in top management and its implications for organizational performance. Conclusions from statistically significant studies show a positive correlation between higher percentages of women in top positions and firm performance (ACCA Pakistan 2010; McKinsey & Co. 2007).

References

ACCA Pakistan (Association of Chartered Certified Accountants Pakistan). 2010. *Gender Diversity on Boards in Pakistan*. Islamabad: ACCA Pakistan.

Heidrick & Struggles. 2010. *Board of Directors Survey 2010*. Washington, DC: Heidrick & Struggles.

McKinsey & Co. 2007. *Women Matter: Gender Diversity, a Corporate Performance Driver.* New York: McKinsey & Co. http://www.europeanpwn.net/files/mckinsey_2007_gender_matters.pdf.

Rhyne, Elisabeth. 2010. "Microfinance, Scale and Financial Inclusion: The End of the Scale Mantra." *Microfinance Insights* 17 (March/April).

Sinha, Francis. 2011. "Beyond 'Ethical' Financial Services." In *New Pathways Out of Poverty*, edited by Sam Daley Harris and Anna Awimbo, 1–53. Sterling, Virginia: Kumarian Press.

State Bank of Pakistan. 2001. *Microfinance Institution Ordinance 2001*. Karachi, Pakistan.

———. 2011. *Strategic Framework for Sustainable Microfinance in Pakistan*. Karachi, Pakistan.

Research Methodology

This study relies on findings from extensive focus group discussions held with women borrowers and field staff of microfinance providers (MFPs). The analysis was supplemented with the following desk reviews:

- Consolidation and analysis of portfolio data of MFPs to obtain information on female borrowers, indicators of portfolio quality by gender, and any other institution-level data that could facilitate analysis and better design of microfinance products. Data for 27 MFPs were collected and analyzed.
- A product-mapping exercise provided an overview of the credit, savings, and insurance products that were being offered in the market and their main features. This exercise also helped to identify products that were specifically designed for, or used by, women entrepreneurs.

The methodology adopted for the fieldwork is described below in detail. The research team worked in the field at three levels: with head offices of select MFPs, with field-level staff of select MFPs, and with women entrepreneurs, most of whom are operating microenterprises.

In-depth interviews with key staff at the head offices of selected MFPs in departments and units dealing with product development, market research, marketing, and operations. The objectives of these interviews were to (1) confirm the data and findings of the product-mapping exercise; (2) explore the organization's strategy toward developing services for women entrepreneurs; (3) identify any products that were designed for, or have been popular with, women entrepreneurs; and (4) understand which product development processes, designs, features, and marketing strategies have, and which have not, been successful in reaching and serving this segment.

Focus group discussions with field-level staff. Previous research and experience have shown that the richest feedback and information often come from this group, which works closely with clients and is on the front lines of MFP efforts. These discussions were used to evaluate how policies designed at the head office level are carried out in the field and validated input from clients. Loan officers

Figure A.1 Sample of Field Staff by Type of Microfinance Provider

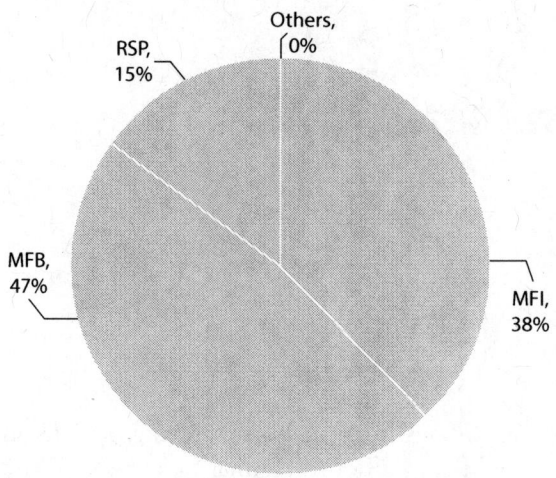

Note: MFB = microfinance bank; MFI = microfinance institution; RSP = rural support program.

have a deep understanding of clients' issues and often belong to the same communities.

Fifteen focus group discussions were organized with 82 members of MFP field staff. Most of these were loan officers and a few were branch managers. Staff of microfinance banks (MFBs) and microfinance institutions (MFIs) collectively made up 85 percent of the total sample (see figure A.1). Forty-four percent were working in rural areas. The breakdown of staff by province was similar to that of clients, with 51 percent working in Punjab, 31 percent in Sindh, and the rest in Khyber-Pakhtunkhwa (KPK), Balochistan, and Gilgit-Baltistan. Unlike client focus group discussions, in which all respondents were women, staff focus group discussions often included both male and female staff.

Focus group discussions with women entrepreneurs were held to get feedback from users of financial services on the products and services that were currently in the market. Two identification strategies were adopted for finding and select-ing participants:

- *Clients of MFPs.* These women were existing borrowers who were identified by their MFPs. Ideally these respondents should have been chosen randomly by the research team and not by the MFP to avoid the institution's choosing only its best clients instead of average clients. The issue for sampling strategy in this case, however, is that not all borrowers are entrepreneurs. Because the focus of this study is the female entrepreneur, it was necessary that those who came to the focus group discussions were in fact running their own businesses. MFPs cannot differentiate between a borrower and an entrepreneur; therefore field-level staff were asked to identify women clients who are entrepreneurs. To counter the bias that might result from MFPs' picking and sending their best entrepreneur clients to the discussions, the research team requested that the complete list of all entrepreneur clients at the selected branch be shared (a listing of names of entrepreneur clients in the branch would suffice), out of which 50 entrepreneurs were randomly selected. Branch staff was then asked to invite any 8 of these 50 for the focus group discussion.

- *Clients of business development service (BDS) providers.* These respondents were identified with assistance of organizations that provide business development services and skills training to women entrepreneurs. There were several advantages to including this group in our sample. Unlike the group who were already clients of MFPs, these entrepreneurs might not use formal financial services. Discussions with this segment of women entrepreneurs would enable them to explain why they do not. Another advantage was the ability to confirm feedback from MFP clients, whose comments might be influenced by the fact that they were contacted by their own MFP to be part of this study.

An alternative to using non-MFPs to seek out women entrepreneurs is to randomly approach such women. Some studies that focus on small and medium-size enterprises and larger businesses use sources like the yellow pages to randomly select such respondents. Because their businesses are so small, women entrepreneurs in Pakistan are unlikely to be listed in such databases or to register with a chamber of commerce or trade union. Therefore the most promising sources of respondents were non-financial-service providers who target this segment with business development or marketing. Attempts were made, however, to randomly approach female entrepreneurs by walking in towns or marketplaces in Lahore and Rajanpur. More walks would have been useful, but the security situation and cultural barriers made them impossible in most areas. In addition, this strategy is appropriate only in areas where there are a large number of entrepreneurs in close proximity.

In all, 33 focus group discussions were conducted with 227 clients. Three clients were interviewed during random walks, and 12 clients were part of focus group discussions related to the floods in 2010. Nearly 50 percent of the clients were identified through BDS providers and the rest primarily through the MFPs. The decision to distribute the sample evenly across BDS clients and MFP clients was based on findings during the pilot focus group discussions. Clients identified through MFPs, especially those that came from less penetrated markets, were influenced by the knowledge that their MFP knew they were part of these discussions and thus would take the time to freely express their opinions. This behavior was less common among mature clients and those living in areas where microfinance penetration is high, such as Lahore and Karachi. Clients identified through BDS providers did not demonstrate this bias and were extremely candid in their feedback and responses.

Figure A.2 shows a breakdown of the sample by type of institution used to identify and gain access to respondents.

Among MFP clients, the distribution of the sample closely matches the distribution of clients by MFP peer groups as reported by the Pakistan Microfinance

Figure A.2 Sample of Focus Group Clients by Source Institution

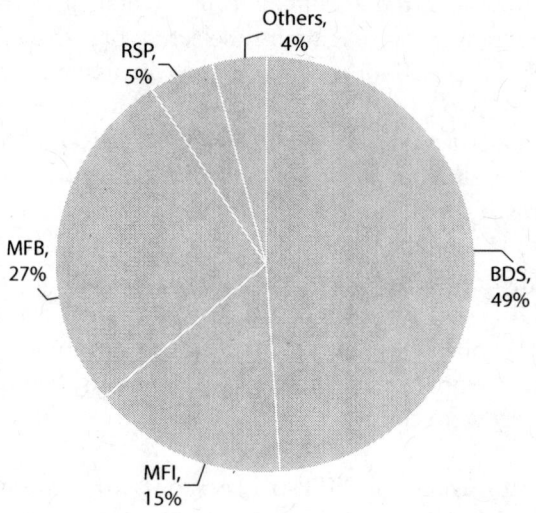

Note: BDS = business development services; MFB = microfinance bank; MFI = microfinance institution; RSP = rural support program.

Network (PMN 2011). The sample is more heavily skewed, however, toward MFBs than rural support programs (RSPs): MFB clients account for 52 percent of sample respondents (out of total MFP respondents) but 40 percent of MFP clients. RSPs account for 10 percent of sample respondents and 23 percent of the MFP clients. There are two reasons for structuring the sample in this way. First, the National Rural Support Programme (NRSP) accounts for over 90 percent of clients of RSPs. Because the products and processes would have been substantially the same, little value would have been added by increasing the number of respondents from RSPs. Second, although most RSPs follow a similar lending methodology, there is more diversification within the MFB peer group. In addition, sector analysts believe that MFBs will become the largest peer group given the transformations of NRSP and the Kashf Foundation from nongovernmental organizations (NGOs) to MFBs.

Selection of Districts

Selection of districts for fieldwork was based on certain premises. The study was designed to be national in scope and cover all provinces of Pakistan. The penetration of microfinance, especially microcredit, was used as a proxy for the level of business activity and potential in a particular area. This assumption is based on the spatial trend of outreach—MFPs expand first in areas most likely to have clients. There is a positive correlation between the presence of MFPs (that is, market penetration) and areas in which the potential market for microfinance is greatest due to higher population density, greater entrepreneurship opportunities, and favorable market conditions (such as access to markets and market infrastructure). Higher penetration would thus mean greater potential for business activity. The likelihood of women being involved in business is higher in areas that have greater economic activity overall. These are also the districts in which microfinance penetration tends to be high.

Distinguishing between rural and urban is problematic in Pakistan.[1] Official rural-urban definitions are based on administrative units rather than the characteristics of the area. Using official definitions is problematic, however, if the issue is understanding the need for and gaps in financial products and services available to rural, as opposed to urban, women entrepreneurs. Whether women entrepreneurs are rural depends on the type of economic activity, mobility constraints, and other area characteristics rather than an administrative designation. Thus, for this study, general characteristics and major economic activities of an area are used to classify it as rural or urban. In addition, lending patterns of MFPs in an area serve as a proxy; regions where agriculture or livestock loans form a major share of the portfolio are considered rural.

Districts with the highest penetration rates in a particular province were generally chosen for fieldwork while also balancing the rural-urban distribution and provincial coverage. Because one of the study objectives was to assess the effectiveness of postcrisis solutions for female microfinance borrowers who suffered from economic and social shocks associated with the 2010 floods, some districts were chosen because they had been affected by the floods and were already areas of microfinance activity. Map A.1 shows the extent of microfinance outreach as of September 30, 2011. Selection of districts by province was determined as follows:

- *Punjab.* Districts of Lahore, Gujranwala, Bahawalpur, Rajanpur, and Dera Ghazi (DG) Khan were chosen in the Punjab. Lahore and Gujranwala are urban centers in central Punjab with high microfinance penetration and substantial female entrepreneurship. Bahawalpur is a primarily rural district in southern Punjab. Focus group discussions with clients in urban Bahawalpur were also conducted to ensure urban coverage from southern Punjab. DG Khan provided the rural sample in central Punjab. Rajanpur was selected for flood-related analysis as it was classified as a "severely affected" district during the 2010 floods.[2]

- *Sindh.* Karachi, Hyderabad, Khairpur, and Sukkur were chosen in Sindh. Of these, Karachi and Hyderabad are urban with penetration levels of microfinance among the highest in the province. Sukkur is a predominantly rural district, and Khairpur is among the districts affected by the 2010 floods.

- *Khyber-Pakhtunkhwa.* Microfinance penetration in provinces of KPK and Balochistan is low due to security concerns as well as geographic and demographic factors. This makes it all the more important, however, to understand the needs of women running businesses in these areas. Peshawar, Abbottabad, and Nowshera were chosen for fieldwork in KPK, of which Peshawar is urban and Nowshera is flood-affected. Rural Abbottabad provided the rural sample

Map A.1 Outreach of Microfinance in Pakistan, 2011

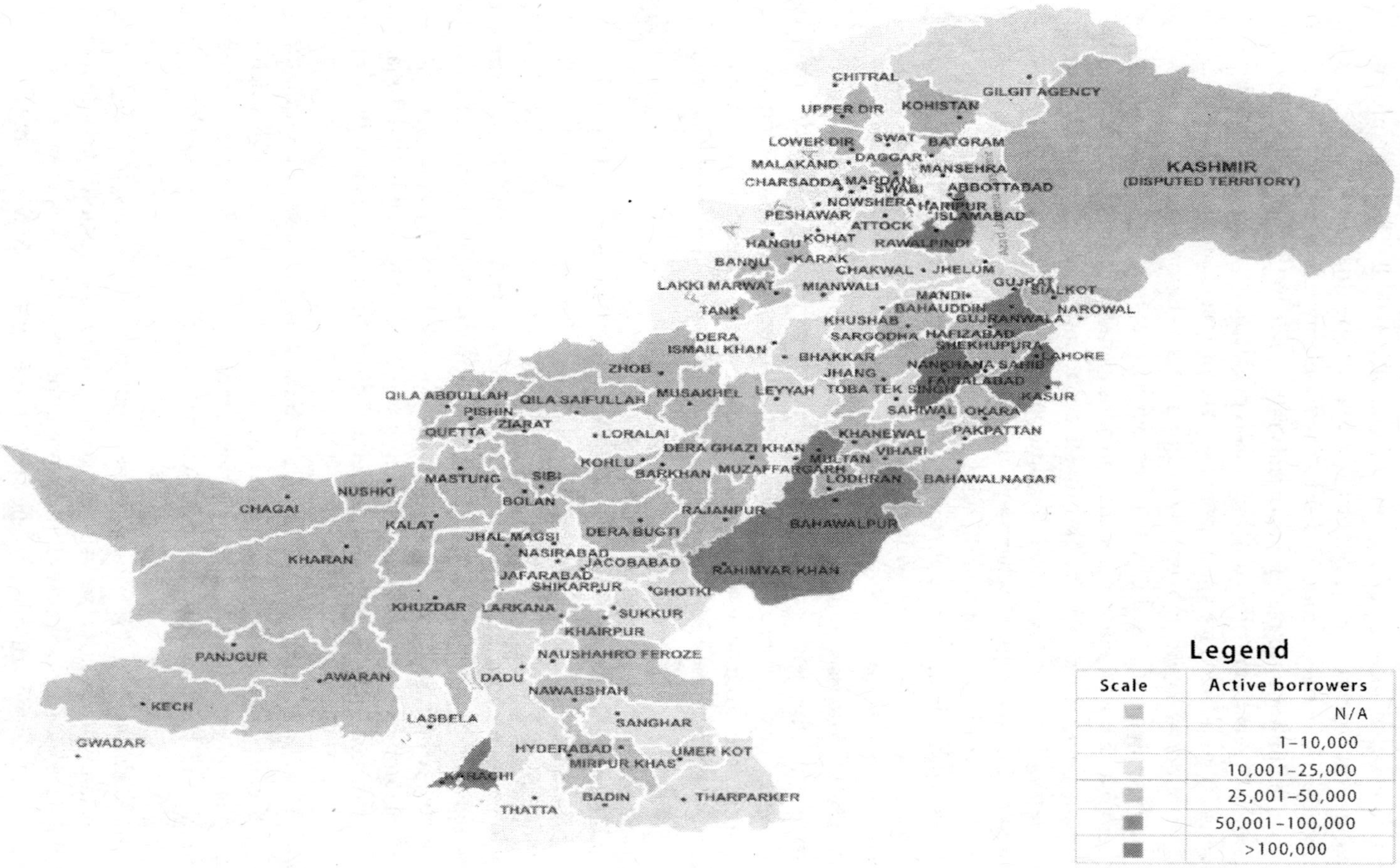

KASHMIR
(DISPUTED TERRITORY)

GILGIT AGENCY

CHITRAL

KOHISTAN

UPPER DIR

LOWER DIR
MALAKAND
DAGGAR
SWAT
BATGRAM
MANSEHRA
CHARSADDA
MARDAN
ABBOTTABAD
PESHAWAR
NOWSHERA
HARIPUR
ISLAMABAD
ATTOCK
RAWALPINDI
HANGU
KOHAT
CHAKWAL
JHELUM
KARAK
MIANWALI
MANDI
GUJRAT
NAROWAL
GUJRANWALA
SARGODHA
HAFIZABAD
NANKANA SAHIB
SHEIKHUPURA
LAHORE
BANNU
LAKKI MARWAT
KHUSHAB
BHAKKAR
JHANG
TOBA TEK SINGH
FAISALABAD
SAHIWAL
OKARA
KASUR
TANK
DERA
ISMAIL KHAN
LEYYAH
MUSAKHEL
KHANEWAL
MULTAN
LODHRAN
VEHARI
PAKPATTAN
ZHOB
QILA SAIFULLAH
LORALAI
KORLU
DERA GHAZI KHAN
MUZAFFARGARH
RAJANPUR
BAHAWALPUR
BAHAWALNAGAR
RAHIMYAR KHAN
PISHIN
QUETTA
ZIARAT
SIBI
BOLAN
JHAL MAGSI
NASIRABAD
JAFARABAD
JACOBABAD
SHIKARPUR
GHOTKI
SUKKUR
KHAIRPUR
NAUSHAHRO FEROZE
MASTUNG
SARKHAN
DERA BUGTI
LARKANA
KALAT
NUSHKI
KHUZDAR
DADU
NAWABSHAH
SANGHAR
UMER KOT
THARPARKER
CHAGAI
KHARAN
LASBELA
KARACHI
HYDERABAD
MIRPUR KHAS
BADIN
THATTA
AWARAN
PANJGUR
KECH
GWADAR

Legend

Scale	Active borrowers
	N/A
	1–10,000
	10,001–25,000
	25,001–50,000
	50,001–100,000
	>100,000

Source: Pakistan Microfinance Network 2013.
Note: N/A = not available.

from KPK. A major issue in KPK and Balochistan is security, which limited the mobility of field teams, especially female staff, and restricted the study to relatively stable districts.

- *Balochistan and Gilgit-Baltistan* (G-B). Quetta (urban) from Balochistan and Gilgit (rural) in G-B were selected. Both have the highest microfinance penetration within the provinces.

One-third of the focus group discussions were conducted in rural areas, and the rest were organized in urban and semi-urban areas. Given the national scope of the study, districts from all five provinces were included. Again, the provincial distribution of the sample follows generally the pattern of microfinance outreach—provinces with a greater share of microfinance penetration had a greater share of the sample of clients (see figure A.3). However, some regions have a greater than proportionate representation in our sample. Directly proportionate representation would have made it very difficult to conduct meaningful analysis or meant no representation of the province in our study. For example, Balochistan represents only 1 percent of microfinance outreach in Pakistan, but respondents from the province make up 7 percent of our sample. Because only two focus group discussions—one with MFP clients and one with BDS clients— were conducted in Balochistan, limiting the participants would have meant no representation from at least one group of clients.

MFP staff attended only one focus group discussion with clients. In general, focus group discussions were held at a neutral location (such as a local hotel) instead of at the MFP branch.

The major MFPs working in the selected districts were identified using PMN's *MicroWATCH*.[3] Institutions were selected to ensure diversity of type

Figure A.3 Distribution of Sample and Microfinance Outreach by Province

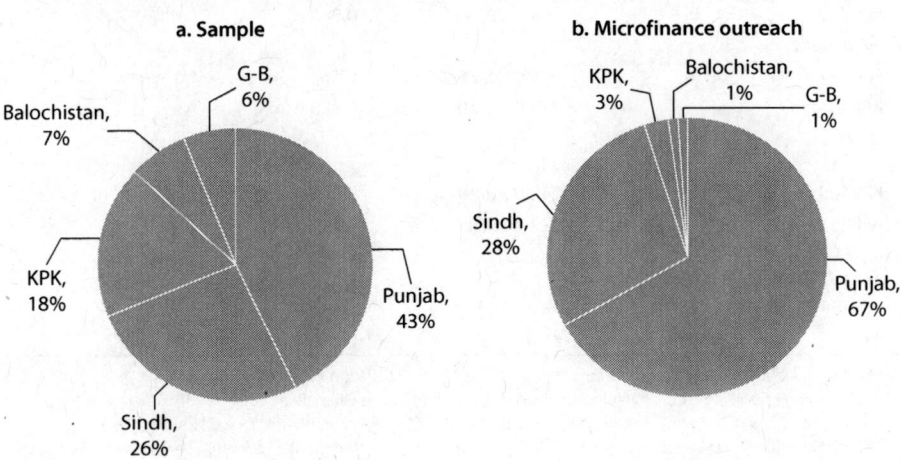

a. Sample

- G-B, 6%
- Balochistan, 7%
- KPK, 18%
- Punjab, 43%
- Sindh, 26%

b. Microfinance outreach

- KPK, 3%
- Balochistan, 1%
- G-B, 1%
- Sindh, 28%
- Punjab, 67%

Note: G-B = Gilgit-Baltistan; KPK = Khyber-Pakhtunkhwa.

(bank, NGO, or rural support program, for example), model (group or individual lending), and innovations such as Islamic microfinance, and branchless banking.

Table A.1 shows the sample distribution by district, MFP, and number of focus group discussions. Thirty-three focus group discussions were conducted with 227 clients. Three clients were interviewed during random walks, and 12 clients participated in focus group discussions related to the 2010 floods. Fifteen focus group discussions were organized with 82 MFP field staff members.

Table A.1 Selected MFPs and BDS Providers by Province

Type of focus group discussion	Urban			Rural		Flood
Punjab sample						
	Lahore	Bahawalpur	Gujranwala	Kasur	DG Khan	Rajanpur
Staff	Kashf (urban)	NRSP Bank (urban)	CWCD (urban)	Akhuwat (semi-urban)	NRSP (rural)	n.a.
MFP clients	Kashf (urban)	NRSP Bank (urban)	CWCD (urban)	Akhuwat (semi-urban)	NRSP (rural)	n.a.
BDS clients	AHAN	AHAN	TEVTA	Karvaan (rural)	n.a.	n.a.
Floods	n.a.	n.a.	n.a.	n.a.	n.a.	NRSP Akhuwat
Random walk	Random walk	n.a.	n.a.	n.a.	n.a.	Random walk
Sindh sample						
	Karachi	Hyderabad	Sukkur	Khairpur	Khairpur	
Staff	Tameer (urban)	Kashf MFB (urban)	ASA (rural)	n.a.	n.a.	
MFP clients	Tameer (urban)	Kashf MFB (urban)	ASA (rural)	FMFB (rural)	n.a.	
BDS clients	n.a.	ECI; ECDI; MEDA	AHAN	n.a.	n.a.	
Floods	n.a.	n.a.	n.a.	n.a.	FMFB	
KPK/Balochistan/FANA sample						
	Peshawar	Quetta	Abbotabad	Gilgit	Nowshera	
Staff	KBL (urban)	n.a.	SRSP (rural)	FMFB (rural)	n.a.	
MFP clients	KBL (urban)	KBL (urban)	SRSP (rural)	FMFB (rural)	n.a.	
BDS clients	AHAN Women Business Incubation Center	MEDA	ECI; AHAN	AKRSP	n.a.	
Floods	n.a.	n.a.	n.a.	n.a.	KBL; SRSP	

Note: AHAN = Aik Hunar Aik Nagar; AKRSP = Aga Khan Rural Support Programme; ASA = Association for Social Advancement; BDS = business development services; CWCD = Centre for Women Co-operative Development; DG Khan = Dera Ghazi Khan; ECDI = Entrepreneurship and Community Development Institute; ECI = Empowerment through Creative Integration; FANA = Federal Administered Northern Areas; FMFB = First MicrofinanceBank; KBL = Khushhali Bank Ltd.; KPK = Khyber-Pakhtunkhwa; MEDA = Mennonite Economic Development Associates; MFP = microfinance provider; NRSP = National Rural Support Programme; TEVTA = Technical Education and Vocational Training Authority; n.a. = not applicable.

Notes

1. Local Government Ordinance 2001 divides areas into zilas, tehsils, towns, unions, villages, and neighborhoods based on the levels at which local government councils were established. These divisions dilute the rural-urban distinction in certain parts of the country. Rural settings are defined as composed of villages: "'Village' means an integrated and contiguous human habitation commonly identified by a name and includes a dhok, chak, killi, goth, gaown, basti or any other comparable habitation" (Local Government Ordinance 2001). For the full text of the Ordinance, see http://www.nrb.gov.pk/publications/Punjab_Local_Government_Ordinance_2001_old.pdf.

2. Source: http://reliefweb.int/sites/reliefweb.int/files/resources/Full_Report_12.pdf.

3. PMN (Pakistan Microfinance Network). 2011. *MicroWATCH* (June).

Clusters of Women-Owned Microbusinesses

Most women entrepreneurs in Pakistan are engaged in traditional business sectors. A traditional business can be one that is an extension of the work that women generally do, such as managing livestock and poultry, or one that employs a skill that is taught by one generation to the next, such as embroidery or crafts-manship. Traditional businesses differ between rural and urban areas. Farm-based businesses are more common in the rural areas; non-farm-based businesses such as embellished fabrics, home textiles, and the beauty sector, are more popular in the urban centers. There also seems to be a greater diversity of businesses in urban areas (especially in the Punjab), a result, perhaps, of access to markets, access to information, and a relatively liberal social setting, all of which allow for more mobility and interactions between men and women. A number of studies that map women-dominated business clusters and value chains have been under-taken by various donors, but their results were not publicly available at the time this study was undertaken. Bringing these into public domain, and supplement-ing them with analyses of additional sectors, could be useful in developing a deeper understanding of women-owned businesses across sectors and whether they require customized solutions and assistance. Although such analysis is beyond the scope of this report, we use existing information to highlight two key clusters in which high participation of women is documented: (1) dairy and (2) handicrafts.

Dairy Sector

The Pakistan Dairy Development Company (PDDC) issued a white paper on the country's dairy sector in June 2006 (PDDC 2006). It envisions a "white" revolution for Pakistan in which the dairy sector will "drive the development of the socio-economic landscape of rural Pakistan" (PDDC 2006, 6). The document envisions a role for microfinance by stating that by the year 2015 "the linkage between the dairy industry and microfinance providers [MFPs] will enhance the living standards of millions of smallholder farmers" (PDDC 2006, 65).

Despite its rapid growth, the dairy sector remains highly informal and fragmented. According to estimates, about 43 percent of households in the dairy sector operate under conditions of subsistence with one or two buffalos or cows, and another 28 percent operate under conditions of near subsistence (see box B.1) with herd sizes ranging from three to four animals. (See table B.1 for a snapshot of ownership patterns and shares of milk production.)

In interviews for this study, the dairy and livestock sectors were cited repeatedly as being especially lucrative and having a large number of female participants. According to Mennonite Economic Development Associates (MEDA), nearly 6 million women are involved in milk production in the Punjab alone (MEDA 2011). However, like most sectors, it appears that women's role in the sector is driven by local traditions and is usually limited to caring for the animals and milking them. Men market and sell the output, enabling them to control the income. This pattern varies across regions—in some areas women market and sell milk and *ghee*, but overall their roles in market-oriented dairy are limited (MEDA 2011).

Box B.1 Pakistan's Dairy Sector

According to the latest available statistics, Pakistan is the fourth-largest milk producing country in the world. An estimated 33.6 billion liters of milk is produced annually from 50 million animals managed by approximately 8 million farming households. Its livestock and agriculture sector contributes over 10 percent to the gross domestic product, and its milk economy represents 27.7 percent of the total value of the agriculture sector. The annual milk production is split 71.1 percent from the rural economy and 29 percent from the urban economy. Only 3 percent of the total production of milk is processed and marketed through formal channels. The remaining 97 percent is distributed through a multilayered system of middlemen. Although currently only a small percentage of milk being processed, the market for ultra-heat-treated milk is growing at a steady rate of 20 percent a year.

Source: PDDC 2006.

Table B.1 Ownership Structure and Production Shares in the Dairy Sector in Pakistan

	Household	*Family*	*Commercial*
Farms	75% of farms producing 30–40% of the milk	24% of farms producing 40–50% of the milk	1% of farms producing 12–20% of the milk
Key characteristics	Small farms; 1–3 animals; source of household income; 50% of milk produced is consumed on the farm and 50% is sold	Work is mainly done by the family; 5–20 animals	Work is mainly done by employees; more than 50 animals
Financial incentive	Selling milk provides daily cash for family needs	Generate an income; pass the farm on to the next generation	Operation of a business; generate return on investment, return to labor

Source: MEDA 2011.

The dairy sector is seasonal. The months of May, June, and July are the slow season in the Punjab, when production and sales drop. During this time dairy farmers look for credit to engage in alternative income-generating activities.

With respect to financial services, discussions during this research and literature review confirm the following:

- The informal sector is the largest source of credit in the dairy sector.
- Even where MFPs are present, borrowing levels for the dairy business tend to be low. The reasons include inappropriately small loans; documentation requirements; a group-based lending model; and high interest rates.
- There is a demand for financial services, including credit, but the financial and nonfinancial costs of engaging with formal finance providers discourage entrepreneurs.
- Many households that engage in the dairy sector also engage in other agricultural activities. They require financial services to meet their agriculture production needs (such as purchase of seeds and urea sprays) as well as life-cycle events.
- Dairy production is considered a by-product of farming in rural households, not a major source of income. In some areas, however, such as Rahim Yar Khan and Bhai Pheru in the central Punjab, where corporate producers have begun to tap into the production capacity of small farmers, there is a new trend toward concentrating on dairy production.

The sector profile has important implications for MFPs:

- The market is large and should expand given the growth rate of the formal market for processed milk. For rural households, formalization of the sector could mean greater profitability and a greater ability to demand and absorb credit, generate savings, and require additional services, such as livestock insurance.
- Middlemen (*dhodhis*) are still the largest source of credit in this sector. Interest in microfinance products is low due to the unsuitability of products and procedures.
- Households involved in dairy at the micro level have more than one source of income, making them less vulnerable to financial shocks and better credit risks.
- Dairy production seems to be a household activity. MFPs should develop products that target both men and women or both, in amounts that range between PRs 50,000 (US$555) and PRs 100,000 (US$1,111), with a repayment period of one year.
- Women also participate in the dairy sector as village milk collectors. These women collect the milk and supply it either to the cities or to a corporate buyer. They often engage in other businesses as well.
- In many cases, the corporate buyer provides the credit or purchases machinery or equipment for the milk collectors and the producers, substituting for both informal and formal sources of credit, such as microfinance.

- Large amounts of dung are generated by commercial-scale dairy farming (such as in the milk colony of Karachi), which could be used for production of biogas. MFPs could explore the possibility of developing products to finance such linked activities.

Handicrafts Sector

The term "handicrafts" encompasses a broad range of activities, especially in Pakistan. The country produces diverse products through skills perfected by men and women over generations. These vary from one region to another, even within the same province. Although the craftsmen and women are quite adept at what they do, they operate for the most part with little understanding of contemporary design and needs. Their products tend to be of low quality (due to the use of cheaper inputs) and outdated in design, and they are unable to be sold at good prices.

A number of organizations have undertaken initiatives to train and assist these craftsmen and women and link them to markets to enable them to increase their incomes and improve their living standards. These include Kaarvan (based in Lahore), Aik Hunar Aik Nagar (AHAN) (based in Lahore, with regional offices in other provinces), and MEDA (based in Islamabad). Most of them provide skills-development training and market exposure services to their beneficiaries; a few provide business development training and services as well. Sector clusters spring up where a number of women in physical proximity engage in similar activities. Clustering enables entrepreneurship development organizations to efficiently design and implement appropriate products for clients. Handicraft clusters in which men have a larger presence are not discussed here.[1]

Note

1. These include carpet making, ajrak (shawl) making, pottery, lacquer work, leather-work, and woodcarving. Using extensive market research, AHAN has developed cluster information reports on 600 nonfarm clusters in 15 product sectors located in four provinces of Pakistan. At the time of writing this report, these cluster information reports were in the process of being published.

References

MEDA (Mennonite Economic Development Associates). 2011. "Understanding Dairy, USAID Entrepreneurs Project." *Pakistan Newsletter* 11 (July–September): 3.

PDDC (Pakistan Dairy Development Company). 2006. *The White Revolution: White Paper on Pakistan's Dairy Sector.* Lahore, Pakistan: PDDC.

List of Persons Consulted in Pakistan

Institution	Name
U.S. Agency for International Development (USAID)	Kanwal Bokharey
United Nations Development Programme	Shakeel Ahmad
International Finance Corporation	Shabana Khawar
Canadian International Development Agency	Sherry Greaves
	Umbreen Baig
European Commission	Rafael Sánchez
Agribusiness Support Fund	Shad Muhammad
Mennonite Economic Development Associates	Fazila Banu Lily
Kaarvan	Ayesha Saifuddin
Empowerment through Creative Integration	Zainab Feroz Kapadia
	Saleem Jehangir
USAID Entrepreneurs	Agnes G. Luz
Women Business Incubation Centre, Small and Medium Enterprise Development Authority	Maimoona Sattar
	Nabila Irfan
Pakistan Poverty Alleviation Fund	Qazi Ismat Isa
	Yasir Ashfaq
	Asghar Ali Memon
	Saqib Siddiqi
State Bank of Pakistan	Dr. Saeed Ahmed

Environmental Benefits Statement

The World Bank is committed to reducing its environmental footprint. In support of this commitment, the Office of the Publisher leverages electronic publishing options and print-on-demand technology, which is located in regional hubs worldwide. Together, these initiatives enable print runs to be lowered and shipping distances decreased, resulting in reduced paper consumption, chemical use, greenhouse gas emissions, and waste.

The Office of the Publisher follows the recommended standards for paper use set by the Green Press Initiative. Whenever possible, books are printed on 50% to 100% postconsumer recycled paper, and at least 50% of the fiber in our book paper is either unbleached or bleached using Totally Chlorine Free (TCF), Processed Chlorine Free (PCF), or Enhanced Elemental Chlorine Free (EECF) processes.

More information about the Bank's environmental philosophy can be found at http://crinfo.worldbank.org/crinfo/environmental_responsibility/index.html.